Mrs. Wayman

Lessons in Comprehension

Explicit Instruction in the Reading Workshop

FRANK SERAFINI

HEINEMANN • PORTSMOUTH, NH

Heinemann
A division of Reed Elsevier Inc.
361 Hanover Street
Portsmouth, NH 03801–3912
www.heinemann.com

Offices and agents throughout the world

Library of Congress Cataloging-in-Publication Data
Serafini, Frank
Lessons in comprehension : explicit instruction in the reading workshop / Frank Serafini.
    p. cm.
  Includes bibliographical references.
  ISBN 0-325-00625-3 (alk. paper)
  1. Reading comprehension. 2. Reading (Elementary). 3. Reading (Middle school).
I. Title.
LB1573.7.S47 2004
372.47—dc22   2004004525

Editor: Lois Bridges
Production: Elizabeth Valway
Cover design: Catherine Hawkes, Cat and Mouse
Cover photo: Jill Moe, Action Photographer
Interior Design: Jenny Jensen Greenleaf
Composition: Publishers' Design and Production Services, Inc.
Manufacturing: Steve Bernier

Printed in the United States of America on acid-free paper
08 07 06 05   ML   4 5

This book is dedicated to my sister,

Suzette Marie Serafini Youngs,

classroom teacher extraordinaire.

Her gentle ways with children, her enthusiasm for literature,

and her dedication to the teaching profession inspire me.

She is the kind of person I always wanted to have for a teacher.

Contents

List of Lessons

Foreword

Frank Serafini has done reading professionals a genuine service in his latest offering, *Lessons in Comprehension: Explicit Instruction in the Reading Workshop.* The service is to help teachers and teacher educators find a pathway to the mecca of "scientifically-based reading research," at least as that standard applies to the teaching of comprehension. An alternative title for the book might be, *How to Make the Science of Teaching Reading Real.* The problem with the research on teaching comprehension is that while it implicates a whole range of explicitly taught strategies as effective in improving students' understanding of texts, it says little about HOW the instruction of those strategies ought to proceed. Hence the reader of a document such as the chapter on text comprehension from the *National Reading Panel Report* is left with an exhortation to "go forward and teach comprehension explicitly," but with little guidance about the nuts and bolts, or for that matter the theoretical grounding, of that explicit instruction. That is where Frank's book enters the picture. What he has done is to embed the explicit teaching of research-documented strategies for understanding text into a set of activity structures (such as think-pair-share, responding to text, reader's theatre, and some three score others) that teachers will recognize from their daily practice, from workshops they have attended, and from professional articles and books they have read. This is intentional on Serafini's part; indeed he admits up front that he wrote this book as a companion to his earlier Heinemann book, *The Reading Workshop,* as a way of guiding readers of the earlier book into explicit instruction.

And he does it admirably. Often, in championing explicit instruction, reading educators talk about "sharing the secrets of our cognitive successes," "making our thinking public," "showing our work," or "demystifying the tools that are typically the province of the educational elite." In short we extol the virtues of making what is typically tacit or implicit in effective reading explicit and open for public examination. In embedding comprehension strategies into the familiar classroom routines encountered in his book, he has accomplished an ironic goal—he has made the explicit implicit rather than making the implicit explicit. He has succeeded in making the scientifically-based strategies that we read about in the national reports and reviews of literature a matter of "routine." In other words, Frank helps us unearth these cognitive secrets by making them commonplace in everyday classroom activities.

Frank's notion of explicitness is complicated and nuanced by this stance. A couple of quotes from his book reveal his true colors in terms of his stance toward teaching and learning. From early in the book (page xiv),

Effective teaching has as much to do with a teacher's ability to respond to the needs of individual readers and his ability to develop a collaborative community of readers, as it does with his ability to create and conduct explicit comprehension lessons.

This tells you that he sees a limited, instrumental role for explicit strategy instruction—that like phonics, it is nothing more than a means to an end, and the end is making meaning in response to text. I concur. Reading strategies are only as good as the meaning kids can make with them. He says as much explicitly in the introduction to Strand 5 of his book:

> Like many of the lessons described throughout this book, we need to be careful that readers don't become focused on the strategies themselves and forget that the purpose is to make sense of what they are reading. (82)

A second plank in his philosophical platform is captured in this quote:

> When teachers are working alongside a student, helping her use different strategies to make sense of a text, or explaining to her some of the criteria successful readers use to choose an appropriate text for independent reading, they are teaching comprehension. (1)

What this suggests is that for Frank explicitness is as much about supporting and scaffolding students in carrying out a strategy—leading from beside and behind if you will—as it is telling and modeling. This is an important insight, one that I readily endorse.

Frank recognizes the potential folly in a book like this—that the examples he provides will become scripts for teachers to follow rather than illustrations of how one teacher managed to teach explicitly. He wants transparency (so it is crystal clear to folks) with prescription. He wants us to avoid what I call the "tyranny of the example," where the rest of us feel as though we have to do it "just like Mike." He does not use the metaphor, but I think it is appropriate to think of the examples he provides as the teaching equivalent of "sourdough starters." You need to have a starter to have any chance of ending up with real sourdough product, but you have to keep adding your own set of "active ingredients" to keep the dough and the starter alive and fresh. Frank wants us to adapt not to adopt his lessons. Wise advice, I think.

Serafini goes out of his way to pay his intellectual debts. From Randy Bomer, he borrows the term *clarity*. From Brian Cambourne, he adapts four continua for characterizing instruction: from explicit to implicit instruction, from mindful to mindless instruction, from systematic to unsystematic instruction, and from contextualized to decontextualized instruction. And from me he adapts the idea of the scaffolding that gets faded as one traverses the scale of the gradual release of responsibility. From these and other sources, he comes up with his own ideal about explicit instruction: it should be deliberate, responsive, clear, and relevant. His driving metaphor for explicit instruction is that it will serve as an "instructional compass" to help young learners stay on course toward meaning and independence as readers.

This is not a theoretical treatise (thank goodness most of you are shouting at this point!!!!), but it is theoretical in its grounding. Lessons are couched in the practical language of instruction, routine, and activity, but the underbelly is highly theoretical and research-based. Another way to think about what Frank has done is to revisit lessons taught under a different guise for a different purpose (e.g., discussing a piece of literature or assessing the relevance of a visual display of information) and then reanalyze those to show that they contain elements of what others call explicit instruction.

You will find some old friends and some new friends as you traverse his lesson landscape. There are the usual suspects, such a summarizing, themes, symbols, and drawing inferences. And they are admirably acquitted. Most of the less familiar lessons come in the last section where Frank flirts with a decidedly critical literacy perspective. And this is where Frank is really in his element. You can sense the shift in register, voice, and enthusiasm when he starts talking about how to unearth stereotypes (especially well-concealed ones), how to provide "official" readings (the kind that get you high scores on tests), how to interrogate advertisements, and how to detect the travesties and the misleading character of basalizing (adapting, amending, and excerpting) trade literature.

You will find your own favorites. Here are mine: asking quality questions, making intertextual connections, understanding purposes for reading, reading visual images and components, evaluating sources of information, responding to our responses, understanding "official" meanings, asking new questions, constructing a classroom library, and What have they done to this story? And unlike the scope and sequence requirements in your basals or the standards list from the state curriculum, Frank does not expect you to use each and every one of these activities every year, and certainly not at any particular point during the year. Think of it as a menu, as a scope without a sequence, as a set of possibilities for developing your very own way of operationalizing scientifically-based comprehension strategy instruction.

When you get Frank's book, pretend that an old friend has sent you your very own comprehension sourdough starter for creating your personal variation of explicit comprehension instruction. And let the baking begin—just remember to try not to turn out any half-baked loaves.

P. David Pearson
Berkeley, California

Introduction

In my first book, *The Reading Workshop* (2001), I dedicated a great deal of space explaining to classroom teachers how they might create an active, caring community of readers. I described in detail how I invited children into the world of reading, made suggestions for exploring the structures and elements of literature, and presented ideas for launching literature study groups. Since its publication, I have often wondered whether I underemphasized the role that explicit reading and comprehension instruction played throughout my reading workshop. I wanted teachers to understand that explicit instruction was an important component of my reading workshop, but only one component of a comprehensive framework for supporting the development of successful, proficient readers.

Whether I was helping children choose books from the classroom library, facilitating a literature study group, demonstrating reading strategies to a small group of readers, or offering advice in a one-to-one reading conference, I was teaching children how to make sense of what they were reading. I wasn't necessarily standing in front of the classroom when I did it, but I was teaching reading. Not a day went by in my years of teaching when I didn't teach a specific lesson, to some particular readers, explicitly and directly. As an intermediate-grade classroom teacher, I taught reading every day, it just didn't always look like the traditional instruction we have come to associate with the teaching of reading.

During my reading workshop, I allocated approximately 25 percent of the total workshop time to reading lessons, a time when I stood in front of my students demonstrating many of the comprehension practices and strategies that proficient readers utilize. The remaining 75 percent of the time was provided for students to practice and apply the things I taught during those reading lessons and to interact with a variety of texts and other readers.

During the past few years, I have had the privilege of working with students and their teachers across the United States. Many of these teachers have begun reading literature and informational texts aloud each day and have incorporated invested discussions of literature into their reading workshops. They are initiating literature study groups, exploring the structures and elements of literature, and assessing readers' growth through observation and various reading assessments. In essence, these teachers have built the foundation upon which explicit comprehension instruction takes place.

Once these various structures of the reading workshop are in place, what many of these teachers want to know is, What did my reading comprehension lessons look like? How did I decide what to include in them? What resources did I use in those lessons? How did I assess their effectiveness? This book is designed to address these questions.

One of the primary challenges I have in sharing my comprehension lessons is to describe what I have done in my classroom as completely as possible without being overly prescriptive. I want to explain in detail how these lessons proceeded. I want to share the reasons I chose to conduct particular lessons. I want to share some of the resources I used. And I want to do all of this without telling teachers what to do each and every day in their classrooms.

The comprehension lessons I share thoughout this book are meant to be adapted to fit your classroom, your objectives, and your students. They are intended as a framework for you to work within, not a set of scripted lessons for you to follow. They are designed to help you develop your own lessons and to encourage you to take charge of your reading instruction program. You are the decision maker. You are the person that knows your students and their needs and interests. You are the knowledgeable teacher. I am just a resource for you to call upon to help you provide the most effective instructional experiences you can.

Effective teachers teach—they don't sit idly by and hope their students will become readers. However, that doesn't mean they dominate the entire day with lectures, nor does it mean the comprehension lessons they provide look like the ones found in the teachers' manuals of commercial reading programs. Effective teaching has as much to do with a teacher's ability to respond to the needs of individual readers and his ability to develop a collaborative community of readers as it does with his ability to create and conduct explicit comprehension lessons.

Comprehension lessons are most effective when they are supported by the structures and experiences provided within a workshop approach to reading instruction. These lessons are not a silver-bullet solution to the challenges of supporting novice readers. Each lesson is intended as a brief description of those instructional experiences that worked for me based on my expectations for the readers in my classroom and the resources available to me.

The lessons we create and the experiences we provide for our students have changed over the years, as surely as the research we have used to develop our lessons has changed. My goal in this book is to place explicit instruction in proper perspective. I want to explain how explicit comprehension instruction fits into the context of the reading workshop so that classroom teachers will realize that these lessons are only one part of a comprehensive reading framework, albeit an essential one.

The Role of Explicit Comprehension Instruction in the Reading Workshop

In the classroom, teaching one set of basics for everyone may appear to be easier for the teacher because the teacher needs to know less, a single routine leaves little room for disagreement and hence may foster obedience to authority.
—ELLEN J. LANGER, *The Power of Mindful Learning*

The reading workshop is a framework for organizing an array of classroom learning experiences. Within this organizational framework, teachers give their students time to engage in reading and encourage them to share their responses to literature and informational texts with each other. The reading workshop framework also provides teachers with numerous opportunities to teach reading. That's right, teach! Explicit, deliberate, preplanned, engaging reading comprehension lessons. Effective teachers teach during the reading workshop, every day, in a variety of settings, for a variety of purposes.

Although comprehension instruction is often thought of as a time when a teacher stands in front of a classroom lecturing to students, delivering the type of one-size-fits-all lessons referred to in the epigraph, comprehension lessons actually take place throughout the entire reading workshop. When teachers are working alongside a student, helping her use different strategies to make sense of a text, or explaining to her some of the criteria successful readers use to choose an appropriate text for independent reading, they are teaching comprehension. However, there were also times in my reading workshop when I did, in fact, stand in front of my students for a brief period of time and demonstrate particular strategies for comprehending texts or procedures to be followed in the reading workshop.

The comprehension lessons I conducted in my reading workshop were preplanned learning experiences that served as an instructional compass, helping my students understand the direction in which we were heading during the reading workshop. These lessons were designed to call students' conscious attention to the various roadblocks, signposts, and challenges up ahead. Simply stated, my comprehension lessons were designed to help readers develop their ability to read.

Explicitness in Comprehension Instruction

It's hard to find the words *reading instruction* in commercial programs and government-sponsored documents without finding an adjective like *explicit, direct, sequential,* or *systematic* attached to them. But what does this really mean? Does it assume that teachers haven't been teaching, or haven't been teaching correctly? Does it mean that the word *instruction* has been expanded to mean too many things, and we have to be more specific in our use of the word? Or does it allude to the idea that comprehension instruction must be controlled through mandated commercial programs in order to be effective?

Particular literacy educators have been advocating explicit, systematic instruction in decoding and comprehension skills for many years. Some envision explicit instruction as a series of required instructional steps or procedures designed to guarantee that students understand exactly what is expected of them and what is being taught. Others are concerned that *explicit instruction* is simply a new label for commercial reading programs that contain tightly structured, scripted lessons. Whatever the case, the word *explicit* keeps popping up and I believe it warrants some discussion before proceeding to other considerations of quality reading comprehension instruction.

Explicit instruction is often considered the opposite of vague, implicit, or embedded instruction. The word *explicit,* when attached to the word *instruction,* implies a more sequential, more rigorous type of instruction when compared with the embedded instruction often associated with workshop approaches to reading comprehension instruction. However, I believe this is misleading. Describing the differences between explicit instruction and embedded instruction on the basis of when the instruction takes place, where it takes place, or the series of instructional steps contained in the lesson may oversimplify some important distinctions. Simply adhering to a series of instructional moves does not guarantee that explicit instruction has taken place. The degree of explicitness in an instructional experience hinges upon the language used in the instructional event and the relationship that is developed between the teacher and the students during the event. What may be very explicit to one student may be quite vague to another. In fact, one could go the other way and be *too* explicit, offering redundant information to students during a comprehension lesson.

Randy Bomer (1998) wrote that explicitness is a focus on the degree of clarity of a particular lesson. The degree of clarity lies in the learner's constructions and deliberate use of a particular concept, strategy, or procedure. His focus was on the learning that took place, not on the degree of explicitness found in the language used by the teacher in the instructional sequence. Whether we have been explicit or not can be assessed only after the learning experience, when we are able to determine if students understood what we taught them. In order to determine whether they have learned the concepts we have taught them, we require learners to demonstrate particular actions or understandings after we have completed the lessons. It is a focus on the learning that has taken place, not simply an evaluation of the language or sequence of procedures in an instructional experience, that determines whether a lesson was explicit or not.

Richard Allington (Allington and Walmsley 1995) describes quality reading comprehension instruction as "active" instruction, the kind of instruction that demands participation from both students and teacher. It involves rational planning, based on close observations of students. For Allington, *explicitness* refers to one's ability to bring to conscious awareness one's learning and reading processes. Based on his suggestions, maybe explicit comprehension instruction should be called wide-awake instruction.

Instruction at the point of use is how Deborah Price (1998) described explicit instruction. She suggested that instruction must be contextualized in the act of reading and should focus on students' needs as they arise. An important aspect of explicit comprehension instruction is the teacher's ability to observe and determine what students need to learn in order to progress as readers. Teachers should not simply follow a script, or as the epigraph indicates, teach one set of basics for everyone; rather, they should adapt the learning experiences and focused engagements in their classroom to fit the needs of individual students.

In addition, Brian Cambourne (1999) has offered a series of four Possible Dimensions of Learning and Teaching for us to consider when we are analyzing our instructional practices and reading comprehension lessons. He discussed the differences between explicit and implicit instruction, mindful and mindless instruction, systematic and unsystematic instruction, and contextualized and decontextualized instruction. He concluded that literacy instruction that is explicit and systematic but also mindless and decontextualized may be dangerous because it makes learning more complex than it ought to be. He also suggested literacy instruction that is mindful and contextualized but also implicit and unsystematic may create serious barriers for many learners. It seems that it has become more complicated than simply whether we are being explicit or not.

For the purposes of this book, I will describe explicit instruction as instruction that focuses on a strategy, practice, or particular aspect of the reading process, calls to conscious attention what is being taught, and strives to clarify for students the expectations we have for their learning. However, whether one is explicit enough is not the only consideration a teacher should address when designing effective comprehension instruction. In addition to being explicit, comprehension lessons should be:

1. *Deliberate*—The teaching that occurs during our comprehension lessons should be deliberate, meaning teachers have a purpose or goal they are trying to achieve. These purposes may range from instilling a love of reading to demonstrating specific comprehension strategies; however, in effective reading lessons, we do set expectations and objectives for our instruction. Comprehension lessons should be rationally planned, meaning that we have legitimate reasons for conducting them and can articulate what these reasons are. Although we must remain cognizant of the ways our students respond to our lessons, we also have to have an idea about where we are headed. Quality comprehension lessons are not haphazard, nor are they a single routine that leaves no room for individual differences.

2. *Responsive*—Comprehension lessons should be created based on observations of our readers, our knowledge of the reading process, and the experiences we can provide in our classrooms. They are designed to respond to what students need next. Although this is not an exact science, we have to base our instruction on what we know about our students. Whether we call this teaching in the zone of proximal development or providing students with their next learning steps, the idea is that teaching is based on students needs' and abilities, reading research, the district

and state curriculum mandates, community expectations, and the teacher's knowledge base and experience, not on a commercial scope and sequence.

3. *Clear*—The language and the demonstrations we use should help clarify to students what we are teaching. In order to do this, we have to ask students if they understand what we are talking about and watch them when they are applying what they have learned. Explicit instruction does not guarantee explicit learning. The more we clarify our intentions, the more we help students understand what we mean, the more effective our comprehension lessons will be. In other words, we need to attend to the language of our instruction, the relationships that develop between the teacher and the learner, and the concept or practice we are teaching.

4. *Relevant*—The comprehension lessons we provide should relate to the types of reading that readers do in the real world, not just in school. Our comprehension lessons need to be applicable in and out of school. Relevance is created when students understand the purposes and objectives of our lessons and understand how they relate to their world and their goals. I believe that we should discontinue doing things in school in the name of literacy education that don't occur anywhere outside the school walls.

5. *Research-Based*—Research should inform our teaching practices and provide information about what really works for our students. Our instructional practices should be based on a wide range of research perspectives and methodologies. We need to be careful that the research base we use to direct our instructional practices is not reduced to such a point that important instructional decisions are based on a single vision of teaching and learning.

The list of characteristics in Figure 1 has been developed from a range of contemporary, rigorous, scientifically based reading research and provides further direction for determining the quality of our reading instruction practices and programs.

Along with considering the degree of explicitness, classroom teachers should design comprehension lessons to be focused and engaging learning experiences that demonstrate particular aspects of reading and being a successful reader. Comprehension lessons are focused instructional opportunities designed to support children's development and growth as readers. In addition to serving as a compass, providing direction for our reading instruction, our comprehension lessons also act as an instructional zoom lens, allowing us to focus in on particular aspects of reading and literacy development at particular times. Our lessons should focus on particular reading strategies, various structures and elements of literature, ways to effectively participate in literature discussions, and new ways to respond to literature.

Not only are effective comprehension lessons focused, but they are also designed to engage students and support their participation in the learning experiences of our reading workshop. Students need to be engaged in our instructional experiences if these experiences are to be beneficial for them. Based on Brian Cambourne's (1988) conditions of learning and engagement, students need to know they will be able to do what we ask, they need to see purpose in what we are doing, and they need to be allowed to make mistakes along the way.

Scientifically based reading research says effective comprehension instruction:

❖ provides opportunities for students to read

❖ integrates reading with other subject areas

❖ focuses on meaning and the process of constructing meaning with the text

❖ helps students understand what it means to be a successful reader

❖ provides opportunities for discussing literature and other texts

❖ depends upon the effectiveness of the teacher, not a particular program

❖ utilizes diverse and flexible grouping patterns

❖ utilizes a wide variety of reading materials

❖ employs explicit instruction in the context of reading

❖ focuses on developing independent, proficient readers

❖ provides demonstrations of reading and comprehension practices

❖ helps readers engage in the experiences of successful readers

❖ is based on a model of emerging expertise

❖ supports readers at the point of need

❖ sees mistakes as opportunities to teach and learn, not habits to be broken

❖ understands the connections between classrooms and the world

❖ promotes the development of a community of readers

FIG. 1
Characteristics of Effective Comprehension Instruction

May be copied for classroom use.
© 2004 by Frank Serafini, from
Lessons in Comprehension.
Portsmouth, NH: Heinemann.

In short, my comprehension lessons are ten- to twenty-minute learning experiences that call students' attention to various aspects of reading, literature, and membership in a community of readers. It is this calling to conscious attention that is the primary purpose of these lessons.

Engaging students in the comprehension lessons we provide can be a challenge. By providing choice and ownership in the experiences of the reading workshop, responding to students' contributions, providing time and opportunities for students to read and discuss literature, and creating authentic instructional experiences, we can support the kinds of readers we want exiting our classroom at the end of the year.

An Emerging-Expertise Model

The comprehension lessons I describe throughout the remainder of this text are based on an emerging-expertise, or gradual-release-of-responsibility, model described by P. David Pearson (1983). Also known as scaffolded instruction, this model of instruction is based on the gradual release of teacher responsibility to students as their expertise begins to emerge. In this model, teachers are responsible for maintaining the quality of the learning experience as novices assume responsibility for their learning and performances. Beginning with teacher demonstrations, moving to guided practices, and ending with students' independent use, the emerging-expertise model supports learners at their point of need and development.

Teachers begin by demonstrating a particular comprehension practice or strategy, using explicit language to make their literate abilities and strategies visible. These demonstrations are designed to help students understand what proficient readers do and are intended to call to conscious attention a particular aspect of comprehension or the reading process. The primary objective is to focus students' attention on what is being demonstrated.

Next, teachers work alongside readers as they attempt to learn and use the practices and strategies the teachers demonstrated. It is like running alongside a child learning to ride a bike. We provide just enough support to keep them from falling as they learn to pedal and balance on their own. In much the same way, teachers maintain the quality of the learning experience by ensuring that readers don't fall because we let go too early, or get bored because we hang on too long. In many ways, we show readers what to do, then work alongside them while they learn to do it.

Finally, as readers accept full responsibility for making sense of texts, they begin to use these strategies and practices independently. We provide students the opportunity to apply the comprehension strategies and practices we have demonstrated in authentic reading events. Through this process, students become legitimate members of our communities of readers.

In addition, I believe that we need to provide occasions for students to reflect on the teaching and learning that have occurred. They need opportunities to discuss how the strategies we have taught worked for them and to address any challenges they may have encountered. During these debriefings, we can attend to any confusions or gaps in understanding that students may have. This time for reflection also helps us assess students' learning and provides information we can use to develop future comprehension lessons.

The discussion about what constitutes a quality comprehension lesson has been going on for decades or longer, and it will most likely continue into the distant future. In this section I tried to address some of the issues involved in that discussion. As the discussion continues, one thing remains certain: effective teachers teach, every day in a variety of formats and contexts. We need to continue to conduct research on the language of instruction and how particular instruction affects students' engagement and learning. It is important to understand how teachers maintain the quality of the learning experience throughout the release of responsibility and how teachers can provide instructional experiences that are not boring, nor confusing. It is sharing our reading lives, making our literate abilities visible, and maintaining the quality of the learning experience as students assume responsibility for their reading that is the basis for the reading comprehension lessons we provide in our classrooms.

How This Book Is Organized

I have organized my comprehension lessons into eight strands. Each of these strands refers to a set of lessons, sometimes taught together, for addressing an important aspect of reading comprehension instruction. Each of the strands is held together by a common theme or focus in the reading workshop. All of the comprehension lessons in each strand are interwoven to build upon one another. Together, these strands represent a significant amount of my yearlong reading curriculum. The comprehension lessons contained in this book address the International Reading Association (IRA) and National Council Teachers of English (NCTE) standards for reading and the language arts. Each individual lesson contains a description and a series of instructional recommendations for teachers to adapt to their particular settings and students.

The eight strands are:

1. Inviting Children into the World of Reading and Literature
2. Exploring the Structures and Components of Literature
3. Navigating Text
4. Promoting Invested Literature Discussions
5. Developing Comprehension Practices
6. Investigating Informational Texts
7. Extending Response to Literature
8. Examining Critical Perspectives

Each of the eight strands contains eight individual lessons that focus on reading comprehension. I begin each strand with a brief description of the type of lessons included and how they fit into my overall reading workshop. The comprehension lessons I describe throughout this book draw upon a variety of instructional approaches, some of which should be familiar to the readers of this text. For example:

* reading aloud
* literature discussions
* creating visual representations of discussions (charts)
* shared reading experiences
* paired reading
* strategy groups or guided reading

Some of the instructional approaches I describe may be new to some readers and are explained in greater detail when they are included in particular lessons. For example:

- ❖ disrupting textual perspectives
- ❖ invested discussion practices
- ❖ literary perspectives
- ❖ think-alouds

The description of each individual comprehension lesson includes the following components:

1. **Title:** a brief label for the comprehension lesson
2. **The Challenge:** observations that indicate whether this particular reading comprehension lesson may be beneficial or appropriate
3. **My Intentions:** the rationale for conducting this lesson
4. **Lesson Overview:** a description of the comprehension lesson or series of lessons and how they operate
5. **How It Might Go:** a narrative explaining how I present the lesson to students; this will include any classroom charts or artifacts the class makes during the activity
6. **Guided Practice:** the learning experiences used to allow students to appropriate the practices or strategies demonstrated with teacher assistance
7. **Closing Comments:** an opportunity for me to include any concerns or ideas that may be important for teachers to consider

In addition to the aforementioned components, I include, where applicable, any charts that I created in my elementary classroom or lists of books and resources that worked well for me in that series of lessons. These are examples taken directly from my classroom and are intended as possibilities, not scripts to be followed.

I have created a literacy website to support the information provided in this text. On the website are numerous resources, booklists, readings, and links to other literacy websites. I refer the reader to the website for more information, especially extended booklists, throughout the series of lessons. The website allows me to constantly update the resources I am providing and add new books and resources as they are made available. The website address is *<http://serafini.nevada.edu>*.

If you have read any of my previous books or articles, you have noticed that I love picture books and advocate their use in the intermediate, middle, and high school classroom. The comprehension lessons in this book will draw heavily upon picture books as a resource as well. I believe picture books are an important resource and well designed for the types of comprehension lessons described in this book. Picture books are generally shorter than chapter books, contain beautiful illustrations, are good examples of quality writing, and entice young readers to interact with them.

Each comprehension lesson in each of the eight strands represents the type of instruction that supported the kinds of readers I was trying to create and nurture through my reading workshop. There are no guarantees that any comprehension lesson, no matter how successful, will transfer to every educational context. It is because of this that I offer these lessons as descriptions and not prescriptions. You, as a classroom teacher or literacy educator, are the decision maker, the negotiator and generator of the reading curriculum. I trust you to make the appropriate adjustments for your students and purposes.

Inviting Children into the World of Reading and Literature

Before we can help students learn how to read, we have to help them understand why they should read. It is our responsibility as teachers of reading to help novice readers see the value of reading and the wonders of literature. We invite children into the world of reading by experiencing literature together, providing ready access to reading materials, creating time and opportunities for students to read, and supporting students as they share their ideas about their readings with other students.

Although these invitational reading lessons occur more frequently during the beginning of the year, they continue throughout the entire school year. We invite children to explore the books we have placed in our classroom library and learn how to make selections that provide each reader with appropriate levels of challenge and support. Throughout the year, we expose students to new genres, authors, titles, and illustrators and invite them to make connections to particular topics and develop literary relationships with favorite authors. Although invitations don't guarantee student engagement, they provide the foundation and opportunity for students to engage with literature.

Inviting students into the world of literature and reading involves establishing expectations for the readers in our classroom, providing extensive opportunities for students to engage in actual reading, developing a community of readers that are willing to generate and share their interpretations with other readers, and helping readers make appropriate choices for their independent reading.

The comprehension lessons in this section include:

1. Setting Expectations for Readers

2. Choosing Appropriate Texts for Independent Reading

3. Understanding Purposes for Reading

4. Classroom Book Awards

5. Constructing a Classroom Library

6. Understanding Genre

7. Becoming a Member of a Community of Readers

8. Establishing a Readers' Bill of Rights

Setting Expectations for Readers

The Challenge: I frequently notice that my students have a very narrow definition of reading and what it means to be a reader. Too often, inexperienced readers focus on oral pronunciation rather than focus on making meaning and interrogating texts.

My Intentions: This series of lessons is designed to help expand inexperienced readers' understanding of the reading process and what proficient readers tend to do when they read. I want readers to understand that reading is a process of making meaning in transaction with texts, not simply the ability to pronounce words quickly and accurately.

Lesson Overview: I begin this series of lessons by describing my reading life to my students. I explain that I am a "simultaneous reader," meaning I always have several novels, magazines, professional texts, music books, and photography journals going at the same time. I explain that I read different texts at different times for different purposes. Next, I read a series of picture books over the following week, beginning with the picture book *Wolf* by Becky Bloom (1999). *Wolf* is a story of a wolf that comes across a farm for educated animals while he is searching for some food. He quickly develops the desire to become a reader and spends time and effort to develop his reading ability in order to become friends with the other animals. Our discussions focus on what the characters in each of the selected picture books do as readers. We begin a chart describing the many characteristics of readers we have discussed from the books and our personal experiences (see Figure L1.1).

How It Might Go: Good morning, Readers! I'm not sure if you know what kind of reader I am, so I want to explain how reading has affected my life. I read everywhere. I read on the stairstepper when I work out and on the beach when I go on vacation. I sometimes read at stoplights, in the bathroom, and during my lunch break. The one thing I have learned is that I read different books at different times for different purposes. I call this simultaneous reading. Some students think that reading is about saying words correctly out loud, or that they can have only one book going at a time until they finish it. This isn't true. Reading is about making sense of texts and making sense of our world. It's also about reading what you want to read when you need to know something or do something. For the next few days, we are going to read a series of picture books that have readers as main characters or discuss ideas about reading. By the time we finish these books, we should have a better understanding about what it means to be a successful reader. Okay? Let's start a chart about what we think being a reader means to us, then we will read the picture book *Wolf,* by Becky Bloom.

Readers:

understand what they read!!!

buy books of their own

don't like to stop reading

don't like to be disturbed when reading

like to read peacefully

like it *quieter* than usual in our classroom

read a lot in their spare time, at home and at school

take care of their books

practice, practice, practice

imagine they are *in* the book

get a movie or images in their heads when they read

finish the books they choose, most of the time

write about what they read

need help learning how to read

take their time

read to others

can talk about what they have read

use the library

share ideas about what they read

recommend books to other readers

use books to find information

Guided Practice: Readers break into pairs and read selections from the collection of books I have provided about readers and reading (see website booklists for books about readers). They bring ideas back to the reading circle to share and discuss.

Closing Comments: As the first few weeks of school progress, I want my students to understand what it means not only to be a reader but to be a writer, a mathematician, and a scientist as well. Each year I develop a motto or classroom slogan for our reading workshop that focuses students' attention on reading as a meaning-making process. I have used slogans like "Reading Is Meaning" and "Reading: Just Make Sense" in the past.

Choosing Appropriate Texts for Independent Reading

The Challenge: One of the biggest challenges for novice readers is selecting texts that are appropriate to read and understand. Sometimes, young readers choose books that are well below their level, sometimes, well above. In general, the toughest task is helping them choose books they can make sense of and not get frustrated with because they are too difficult. I don't want students to become frustrated with reading, nor do I want them to choose books they cannot understand.

My Intentions: This series of lessons is designed to give students some strategies for monitoring their selections for independent reading and helping them make more appropriate choices. I want students to assume the responsibility for selecting texts themselves rather than choose books for them or level the books in my library. We should allow our readers to choose the books they read, as long as they are making appropriate choices. In order for students to make appropriate selections, they have to understand that reading is making sense of texts and use some of the strategies in this lesson to judge the complexity of their reading material.

Lesson Overview: I select a college textbook in an area that I am unfamiliar with (e. g., astrophysics or geology) and read aloud a brief selection from it. I want students to know that there are books that I don't understand, and that the reason I don't understand them is because I am not experienced with that subject, not because I am stupid. I use this demonstration to lead us to a discussion about how to know when a book is *outside our experience* (I like that way of talking about choosing books, rather than saying some books are *too hard*). I demonstrate how I select books from the library and then ask students to share how they select books. Together, we create a chart with book-selecting tips (see Figure L1.2).

How It Might Go: Good morning, Readers! Remember last week when we talked about what reading is? [Students respond: Making sense and understanding what you read.] Well, it's really important that we make appropriate selections when we read, or we may have trouble making sense of the books or texts we have chosen. Did you know that books will wait around until you are ready to read them? When I was in first grade, there was this one cool book about dinosaurs in the school library that I always wanted to read. I checked it out and looked at the pictures, but I couldn't understand the words at all. Well, by the time I got into fifth grade, I had read this book so many times that I practically knew it

FIG. L1.2
How to Choose a Book

May be copied for classroom use.
© 2004 by Frank Serafini, from
Lessons in Comprehension.
Portsmouth, NH: Heinemann.

❖ Open to any page and see if you can read a couple of paragraphs.

❖ Read what is on the back cover.

❖ Ask friends for ideas.

❖ Look at the table of contents or introduction.

❖ Look at the suggested age level.

❖ Look for favorite authors or genres.

❖ Look through the illustrations.

❖ Read the title and look at the cover.

❖ Ask your teacher for help.

❖ Stop reading after a page and think about what has happened.

Always ask yourself: Can I understand this book?

by heart. I just had to wait until I had more experience reading before I could check that book out and understand it. Are there any books like that for you? Do you have any books you really want to read but know they are too hard right now? [Brief discussion.] Let's just say that some books are outside of our experience.

In order to pick out books that are just right, what can we do? How do you know when a book is right for you? Let's create a chart of our ideas (see Figure L1.2).

Guided Practice: After creating our chart and discussing how to make appropriate choices for independent reading, I ask students to go to the classroom library and choose a book they think is appropriate. While they are sitting and reading, I roam around and see what they have chosen. I discuss, confidentially, each student's choice so as not to embarrass anyone who may have chosen inappropriately. I constantly monitor students' choices throughout the year. I pay closer attention to those students that I feel are selecting inappropriately. Using weekly reading conferences or "reading roll call," I keep track of what each student is reading each day. Reading roll call is like Nancie Atwell's status of the class idea, which she used in *In the Middle*. Instead of calling roll, or taking a status of the class before writing workshop, I do it at the end of the day when I dismiss my students. I use our classroom library checkout cards to call each student's name. Students tell me what book they are reading for homework and one thing that happened the last time they read. This helps them keep track of their reading and ensures they have their book ready to go home each day. Students also write in their literature response logs each evening, and I can monitor their choices through that assignment as well.

Closing Comments: Students have to understand that reading is about understanding and making sense before they will appropriately select books every time. As a reading teacher, my job is to monitor what my students are choosing, not choose books for them. I may make suggestions, but these suggestions are between two readers, not between a teacher and his student. When inexperienced readers are choosing picture books or expository texts that convey information through illustrations as well as written language, we can't assume students need to read every word in order to get something from the text, especially if students have a great deal of background knowledge on the subject of the text. However, I don't want them spending all of their reading time attending to illustrations and not the written text. I know there are social pressures to choose harder books (e.g., chapter books) in many intermediate grades. I have to ensure that the readers in my class can choose appropriately without being embarrassed about their level of experience. Finally, I know that *why we read* greatly affects what we choose. Skimming through the illustrations of an informational text can be appropriate reading sometimes.

Understanding Purposes for Reading

The Challenge: Novice readers often approach a variety of texts in the same manner, with the same expectations. The literary and cognitive strategies necessary for understanding and appreciating poetry, for example, are vastly different than those required to understand and appreciate expository texts. Readers need to understand their purposes for reading and how they affect the strategies and practices they bring to the reading event.

My Intentions: By helping students understand the various purposes readers set for reading different texts in a variety of contexts, we can help them monitor whether their reading experiences have met the purposes they have set, or those purposes that have been set for them in school. I want students to be able to articulate their reasons for reading and evaluate whether their goals have been met by the reading event.

Lesson Overview: This reading lesson will present students with a variety of texts and a variety of expectations for reading. We will begin by charting the various reasons we read and some of the reasons teachers make students read in school. The objective is to help students understand their purposes for reading and use appropriate strategies to meet those goals.

How It Might Go: Good morning, Readers! I am going to ask a question that may seem silly. Let me ask you, Why do we read? Seriously! Why do we choose certain books or magazines or other things to read, and what do we hope to get out of it? (See Figure L1.3 for our class chart.) When I am reading a manual for operating my DVD player or a new electronic gadget, I don't read the same way as when I am reading a novel on the beach during my vacations. I have different purposes for reading each of these texts, so I read them differently. Do you ever think about why you are reading something, or do you just start reading? [Discussion.] Sometimes we just start reading because it is so obvious why we are doing it. I do that, too. I don't always sit around and think to myself, "Okay, Frank, why did you pick up that book, or why are you reading that magazine?" I just do it. But, if someone asks me why I am reading, I should be able to tell them, don't you think? So for awhile, we are going to stop and ask ourselves why we are reading certain things. I want to then discuss how this affects how we are reading and see if we can make a chart of the different *ways* we read texts.

❖ to learn things

❖ for enjoyment, because it's fun

❖ to practice reading

❖ to escape to new places

❖ to get information

❖ to go on an adventure with a favorite character

❖ to dream or imagine new things

❖ to understand ourselves and the world better

❖ for instructions or directions

❖ to build or cook things

❖ to learn about other people

❖ to keep up with important events

❖ to know what to do on the weekend

❖ to know what to wear outside

❖ to get scared

Guided Practice: In the beginning of the year, I ask students to start each entry in their literature response logs by writing down why they are reading what they are reading. I come around during the reading workshop time and ask students from time to time why they are reading something and how that affects how they are reading.

Closing Comments: One way to demonstrate the ideas of this lesson is to use an informational text and a piece of historical fiction and show how each can be read in different ways. If you think your readers can understand them, you may want to introduce Louise Rosenblatt's terms *efferent* and *aesthetic*. Your class can discuss how a text can be read either way, regardless of the genre. I want my students to be able to read both efferently (to carry away information) and aesthetically (to live through the reading event).

Classroom Book Awards

The Challenge: Children need to develop a more sophisticated criteria for what counts as quality literature. Although all types of literature are used in the reading workshop, from pop culture to the classics, the discussion of the characteristics of quality writing and stories is an important one. Just because it's published doesn't mean it's worth reading. Placing an award emblem on a piece of children's literature doesn't guarantee that all children will love the book; however, it does represent our profession's indication of quality reading material. Without adopting an elitist position, having classroom discussions about what our favorite books are, why they are our favorites, and the criteria used by a variety of literary awards is beneficial in helping students develop a discerning palette for their reading tastes.

My Intentions: To investigate the criteria used by children's literature literary award committees and create a system for nominating and awarding a classroom book award for our library selections.

Lesson Overview: Using the criteria for the Newbery, Caldecott, Coretta Scott King, Orbis Pictus, and other literary awards presented to children's authors and illustrators, students create categories for classroom book awards and the procedures and criteria for making the designations. My students in the past have created their own book stickers and names for the awards. These stickers represent students' favorites and their own definition of quality literature. By monitoring their selections and discussing the criteria used to make these selections, we can help children analyze literature and read with more understanding. In addition, we often use the criteria we develop through our discussions in our reading workshop as a rubric during our writing workshop to examine the quality of our own writing.

How It Might Go: Good morning, Readers! I was wondering if any of you have noticed the gold and silver emblems that are on some of the books we have in our library? Do any of you know what these are used for? I think it might be important for us to take a closer look at what these awards are and how they are given out. We need to find out who gives the awards and why they are given. [Have several award-winning books available for investigation.] After we make a list of all the awards that we can find, I am going to assign a small group of students to investigate what each individual award is for and how it is awarded. You can use the Internet or some of the library reference materials that I have checked out for you to find information. When we are finished doing this inquiry project, we are going to create some awards of our own, nominate some books for these awards, and give them out each month for the rest of the year. We will have to decide on the categories we want to give awards for and what the award should look like. [Here I have students brainstorm all the possible categories we could award books for, such as funniest book, best illustrations, most unusual topic.] After we decide on the categories, we will have to decide on how to nominate and award the books. We will also have to make a nice display area in our library to show off our awards. Okay?

Guided Practice: Each small group will be responsible for investigating a particular award. The Internet is an important resource, as well as books about the individual awards. I have used a form to help students find important information (see Figure L1.4).

Closing Comments: This has been an enjoyable process for many years in my classroom. Each year students create unusual and interesting awards. One year we had the Call-d-Cat award that used a Garfield the Cat face for the award. We have had "New Berries" and many other funny names for awards. The most important part of this process is not necessarily the award, but the discussions that focus on what constitutes a quality piece of literature. It is important to assign a group of students to keep up with the monthly nominations or the whole process can be quickly forgotten. If you make each month's designation of the award an important event and create a visually appealing display area in the classroom library, students will be more likely to make this an important ritual in the life of the classroom.

FIG. L1.4
Award Investigation Guide

May be copied for classroom use.
© 2004 by Frank Serafini, from
Lessons in Comprehension.
Portsmouth, NH: Heinemann.

Each group should try to find information in the following areas:

1. Where did the name of the award come from?
2. What group or organization gives out the award?
3. Who decides who wins the award? A committee? A single person?
4. What criteria do they use to give the award?
5. What books have won the award for the past ten years?
6. What else is important to know?

Constructing a Classroom Library

The Challenge: Putting together a classroom library that is inviting, is easy to access, has a predictable organization, allows students to check out books without teacher assistance, and can be maintained by students throughout the year is a challenge. Students need to learn how to take care of the limited collections of books we make available. In order to do so, and to support their trips to the school and public libraries, I think it is also important for students to understand how professional libraries are organized.

My Intentions: To allow students to construct and maintain the classroom library with teacher assistance. I want students involved in every aspect of the classroom library, from initial setup to checkout procedures. I believe that when students are deeply involved with the classroom library, they take better care of our books and the library becomes more inviting.

Lesson Overview: At the end of each school year, I spend a few hours dismantling my classroom library, removing stickers from books and packaging them up for the summer. Before the next year begins, I store my books in large boxes, randomly mixing genres and book formats so my new class can discover the treasures that lie within. I do this because it is important for each class to decide how the library will be organized and take part in its construction.

How It Might Go: Good morning, Readers! As you probably noticed when you came in this morning [probably the first day of school], there are fifteen large boxes, wrapped in Happy Birthday paper, in the corner of the room. Well, today is our library's birthday! We are going to "give birth" to our library today. Each day, for the next three weeks [fifteen days = fifteen boxes], we are going to unwrap a new box and see what reading materials are in there. Each box has all kinds of picture books, chapter books, magazines, and other reading materials. We are going to put all of the texts from one box each day on the six tables in our room and spend some time at each table exploring what we find. We will go around the tables in small groups and take five minutes or so at each table to see what is available. As we are looking at the books, I want you to keep track of what kinds of reading material you find. We will put our ideas up on the large piece of butcher paper I have hung on our back wall (see Figure L1.5 for final list of book types). When we are finished we will do some things with the list, but for now just concentrate on what kinds of reading material you find at each table.

FIG. L1.5
Types of Reading Material Found in Our Library Boxes

May be copied for classroom use.
© 2004 by Frank Serafini, from
Lessons in Comprehension.
Portsmouth, NH: Heinemann.

❖ animal books

❖ poems

❖ books with patterns

❖ Dr. Seuss books

❖ books about space and science

❖ books for really young readers (baby books)

❖ books about friendship

❖ funny books

❖ books about families

❖ books about different countries

❖ books about history

❖ dinosaur books

❖ books with math problems

❖ fairy tales

❖ books about rocks

❖ books about famous people

❖ books about famous places

❖ books about kids today and school

❖ books about things to do and experiments

❖ books about art and artists

❖ books about the way things work

❖ magazines

Guided Practice: I place students in groups of five or six and allow them about five minutes at each table to explore the stack of books. There are pens and Post-its at each table and students write down what they find and stick their ideas on a sheet of butcher paper hung on the wall. Using Post-its allows us to move the types of books students identify into categories later on. I work alongside students as they try to describe and label what kind of reading materials they are finding. The categories we develop will be help us organize our library.

Closing Comments: As this lesson progresses, I discuss what makes a good category for a library. I talk about categories that are too big, like picture books, and categories that are too small, for example, books about ants. It's the Goldilocks Theory of Library Organization: we want to find categories that are just right for the reading materials we have in our classroom. The process of deciding what makes a good category is more important than the actual categories we end up with. During the first few weeks of school, we negotiate the categories and procedures that we will use throughout the year in our library.

One of the most important outcomes of this process is that each student touches almost every book *before* we put it into our classroom library. During this experience, students can write down in their writer's notebooks the names of interesting titles or favorite authors and illustrators they want to eventually read. This is very important. Too often, students don't take the time, or aren't given the time, to explore what is in classroom libraries. One of our jobs is to help young readers find those books that they don't know about yet but will love when they discover them.

Understanding Genre

The Challenge: Many students rarely pay attention to the different sections of the library and how it is organized. They know where their favorite books are located but often do not take the time to explore other areas of the library or different types of books. Exposing novice readers to new genres and types of reading materials is a primary responsibility of the reading or classroom teacher. Understanding the characteristics of various genres helps readers make sense of their reading and supports them in making better choices for their independent reading. I want students to read widely across genres and formats as they become more experienced readers. In order to do so, it is important for readers to know what genres are and what genres are available in the classroom, school, and public libraries.

My Intentions: To help students construct an understanding of the concept of genre and establish a working definition for the most common genres in our library collection.

Lesson Overview: This lesson builds upon the discussions in the Constructing a Classroom Library lesson (see Lesson 1.5). I use the initial chart we constructed as we were exploring the boxes of library books in our room to do a list-group-label exercise in order to create categories for our library. We list out all the types of books we find in the library boxes, then group them together, and, finally, create a label for each group, or category. Most often, each of these categories is a particular literary genre. The process of generating these labels provides a wonderful opportunity to discuss the idea of genre and how libraries are organized.

How It Might Go: Good morning, Readers! Let's take a look at the chart we created from our exploration of the book boxes over the past few weeks (see Figure L1.6). We spent a lot of time trying to find out what kinds of books were in those boxes, didn't we? Now let's take a look at the chart and maybe we can start to see what kinds of books might go together. Of all the kinds of books that you see listed on the chart, do any seem to go together? Which ones are similar to other ones? I am going to ask you to get into small groups to work together to create some categories for our library collection. Okay?

FIG. L1.6
Genres in Our Classroom Library

May be copied for classroom use.
© 2004 by Frank Serafini, from
Lessons in Comprehension.
Portsmouth, NH: Heinemann.

❖ historical fiction

❖ contemporary realistic fiction

❖ science books

❖ art books

❖ humorous books

❖ family stories

❖ social sciences—geography, history, cultures

❖ pattern books

❖ book for young readers

❖ chapter book sets

❖ magazines

❖ brochures and other things

❖ Chris Van Allsburg books

❖ William Steig books

❖ fairy tales and folktales

❖ biographies

❖ science fiction and fantasy

❖ poetry

❖ books about building community

❖ Caldecott winners

❖ postmodern picture books

❖ math workshop books

Guided Practice: In small groups, students get together and discuss the kinds of books that might go together and then create a label for that group of books. After doing this, I have the school librarian visit our class and talk about the way the school library is organized and what categories are available there. For homework over the next few days, I ask students to visit a bookstore, a video store, or a public library to see how it is organized and what categories are used to group its collections. Students bring back lists of the categories they find and we discuss the concept of genre based on what they have experienced and the categories we have created from our wall chart.

Based on the categories we generate, we move the Post-its around until we feel we have a manageable number of categories that we could find boxes or shelf space for. We discuss what kinds of books are in each category and what would be an appropriate label for each category. This is where the word *genre* comes up and students begin to use various terms to describe the categories included in our chart. I introduce names for many of the genres, for example, historical fiction, contemporary realistic fiction, folktales, and cumulative stories, to help describe the categories we have created. We then use these as labels for our boxes.

Closing Comments: The various genres we use to label our boxes come from the students themselves and the books in my library collection, instead of being abstractly constructed and presented to students. My role is to help name the categories we have created, not to define each genre for them. Each year, particular books blur the boundaries between genres, for example, the Magic School Bus series. Is it fiction or nonfiction? Where do we put Chris Van Allsburg books? Or William Steig books? These anomalies create opportunities to help further define genres and help students understand that some books could fit into many of the categories we have created. The power of this is in the discussions, not in the final categories we use to organize our library.

Becoming a Member of a Community of Readers

The Challenge: Readers become readers within a community of readers. In other words, we learn from the company we keep. If we want children to become readers, they need to spend time in the company of other readers and envision themselves as readers. The way students talk to each other and treat each other as readers has as much impact on their success as readers as the lessons we create. Because of this, it is important to pay close attention to the interactions among students, teachers, and texts. It is also important to make the rules, norms, and expectations for our students *visible* so we can talk about them and change them as necessary. In order for students to construct, share, and negotiate understandings about what they read, they have to be able to talk to each other with respect and listen to each other's ideas. Making sense of texts is a human experience that develops within a community of readers.

My Intentions: I designed this series of lessons and discussions to help students understand their role as members of a community of readers. By creating experiences and opportunities for discussing our roles as community members, we are helping students understand how each person contributes to our reading family. I have particular expectations that I share with my students and students have expectations that have been created through their experiences in school. We negotiate these as we explore what it means to be a reader and a member of our community.

Lesson Overview: By reading a series of books about building community (books about friendship, bullies, being an individual, being different, caring, working together, growing up), we discuss throughout the first few weeks of school what it means to be a member of our particular community of readers. (See my website booklists for books about community.)

How It Might Go: Good morning, Readers! We have a lot of students in our class this year and not a lot of space to spend our days. Because of this, it is important that we learn to live together in this crowded space. Ever since civilization began, people have been making rules and laws that explain how they want people to treat each other. In school, you usually come in the first day and the teacher gives you a set of rules to follow, right? Well, not this year. I have a simple set of expectations that I would like to share with you (see Figure L1.7). Does any body know what an expectation is? [Discussion.] Let's take a look at my list and then I am going to read you a book called *Tacky the Penguin*, by Helen Lester (1990). Each day for the next few weeks, we are going to read a new picture book that deals with

25

FIG. L1.7
Community Expectations

May be copied for classroom use.
© 2004 by Frank Serafini, from
Lessons in Comprehension.
Portsmouth, NH: Heinemann.

❖ Think.

❖ Say what you think (appropriately).

❖ Act safely.

❖ Enjoy learning.

❖ Include everyone.

❖ Care about what you do and about your classmates.

being a member of a community, being an individual, or appreciating others. As we read each book, we are going to add to our list of ideas about what we think will help us create a community that will support each of us as an individual reader. Let's take a look at my list of expectations.

Closing Comments: I have gathered together many picture books that address being an individual. I create a slogan each year that describes my expectation for the year. One of my favorites has been "Living Together, Differently." It explains that we can be individuals and still be members of our community. In addition, I often begin the year reading a chapter book aloud that addresses the issue of community. One of my favorites is *Dominic*, by William Steig (1972). In this story, Dominic is a unique dog that always takes the road to adventure. This is one of the messages I want my students to take with them when they leave our community.

The other "rules" needed for a class to operate are created and negotiated with my students as the year progresses. We create a list from our readings and refer to it for our problem-solving meetings and discussions. Our classroom rules and expectations are not imposed, but created together, the same way our community of readers is established.

Establishing a Readers' Bill of Rights

The Challenge: Students have been socialized into particular ways of reading by their experiences in and out of school. Some of these experiences support young children's understandings of what it means to be a successful reader—one who constructs, shares, and negotiates meanings in transactions with texts—and some of their experiences narrow their perspective on what readers do and what it means to read.

My Intentions: This series of lessons is designed to help students understand their roles as readers in my classroom and establish a Readers' Bill of Rights that they can count on throughout our time together.

Lesson Overview: I begin by asking students what they would like to be able to do as readers and then share with them a set of readers' rights that Daniel Pennac put forth in his book *Better Than Life* (1999). It is very interesting coming to know what young readers say they can do as readers and what they think teachers and school experiences expect from them.

How It Might Go: Good morning, Readers! Have any of you ever heard of the Bill of Rights? [Discussion.] If you haven't, it's a document written by our founding fathers about the rights of every American. Well, today we are going to discuss *your* rights as a reader in this classroom. Did you know you have certain rights just because you are here in our room this year? Well, you do. For example, you have the right to check out books from the library to read. How's that? You also have the right to talk about what you have read. As a matter of fact, I expect you to talk about the things you are reading because I am interested in what you think. Really! I mean, I really want to know what you think about the books we read together and the ones you choose to read on your own. Even if you don't like a book, I want you to tell me why you don't like it. It's important in our community of readers that we establish some rights for readers and talk about what we want to be able to do as readers all year long.

Guided Practice: Students begin this lesson by discussing what rights they would like to have. The only right from Pennac's list that I will not allow is the right to *not* read. This is a readers' bill of rights, not a nonreaders' bill of rights. All other suggestions are discussed and negotiated.

Closing Comments: Creating a democratic process in the classroom is one of the most important components of building a community of readers. Along with our rights as readers, we also discuss our responsibilities as readers. I have included the readers' rights and readers' responsibilities that my class created during my last year of classroom teaching (see Figures L1.8a and L1.8b). These rights and responsibilities work only if we pay attention to them and remind students of what they are throughout the year. Over the years, I have prominently displayed these charts on the walls of my classroom in an elementary school.

The right to:

❖ check out books from the classroom and school libraries

❖ read anything we want on Fridays

❖ talk about what we read

❖ not defend our tastes in what we read

❖ have one night a week of no reading homework, if we want

❖ follow along with chapter book read-alouds in our own copy of the book

❖ read any book after it has been read aloud

❖ return books to the library that are too difficult

❖ make suggestions about what books Dr. Serafini will read aloud

❖ read our own books at home and at school

❖ read Harry Potter books

❖ decorate the library and bookshelves

❖ use approximated spelling in our literature response logs

❖ share our literature response logs with a buddy

❖ read in pairs

❖ listen to books on tape in the listening center

❖ have Dr. Serafini read our response logs and write back to us

❖ be heard in literature discussions

FIG. L1.8B
Readers' Responsibilities

May be copied for classroom use.
© 2004 by Frank Serafini, from
Lessons in Comprehension.
Portsmouth, NH: Heinemann.

We are responsible for:

❖ reading six nights a week and in school during reading workshop

❖ writing in our literature response logs five times a week

❖ keeping the library organized

❖ taking care of the books we check out

❖ checking out all books on our library checkout cards

❖ making sense of what we read

❖ listening to others in literature discussions

❖ generating and sharing ideas about what we read

❖ keeping artifacts in our portfolios about our lives as readers

❖ making other readers feel like members of our community of readers

Exploring the Structures and Components of Literature

Literature contains particular elements that authors and illustrators use to create stories. In order for students to understand literature, and to be able to appreciate the craft and style of particular authors and illustrators, we have to explore how literature is created and designed. Various components, for example, plot, theme, symbols, and mood, help readers make meaning as they read. These components are the building blocks of literature and serve as a literary compass, helping readers find their way through a piece of literature.

In addition to the cognitive strategies readers utilize to comprehend texts, this series of lessons focuses on the literary strategies readers need to understand the structures and components of literary texts. These literary strategies offer additional support for readers' transactions with literature.

It is important to stress the point that we cannot allow the study of these components to become an end in itself. Our goal is not to help students quickly identify plots, characters, and themes; rather, it is to help readers use these literary structures and components to construct more sophisticated interpretations of the literature they encounter.

The comprehension lessons in this section include:

1. The Hero Cycle
2. Using Diagrams to Understand Story Structures
3. Central Tensions and Resolutions
4. Interplay Between Text and Illustrations
5. Point of View
6. Themes
7. Symbols and Symbolism
8. Mood

The Hero Cycle

The Challenge: Many students are able to understand the elements of literature, such as plot, setting, character, and theme, but are not able to envision the structure of a story as a whole. Understanding particular story structures, or story grammars, helps readers comprehend stories, relate stories to their experiences, and make connections to other pieces of literature.

My Intentions: This lesson will help demonstrate examples of fictional stories from Western culture that are structured around what Aristotle called the hero cycle. I chose literature and designed a flowchart to call students' attention to the hero cycle, or the home-away-home structure, of many children's stories.

Lesson Overview: I begin by reading the classic children's picture book *Where the Wild Things Are*, by Maurice Sendak (1963). I show the class how the story can be thought of as a cycle of events, beginning with Max being sent to his room and ending when he returns and finds his supper waiting for him. I present a flowchart of the hero cycle (see Figure L2.1) and talk about the different stages of the cycle and how *Where the Wild Things Are* fits this pattern.

How It Might Go: Good morning, Readers! Today we are going to talk about a story structure that has been around for about three thousand years! A Greek man named Aristotle realized that many of the stories of his time were adventure stories in which a hero or heroine went out into the world to solve a problem and came home changed and usually smarter. First, I am going to read *Where the Wild Things Are* again. Yes, I know we have read it many times before, but we are going to look at it differently this time. I am going to stop along the way and fill in a chart called the Hero Cycle as we read. Notice the boxes on the chart. It's called a flowchart. Businesspeople sometimes use flowcharts to keep track of their products and how their company operates. We are going to start with the first box and write "Max at Home" in the box because that is where the story begins. [Read aloud the rest of the story and fill in the boxes on the chart]. Well, what do you think about this chart now? [Discuss chart.]

Guided Practice: Have students in small groups read from selected picture books (see list on Escaping Reality on website) and create hero cycle charts of their stories. Roam around to various groups and monitor their understanding of the hero cycle. Come back together for a discussion of the various stories. Share the charts each small group created.

Closing Comments: I chose *Where the Wild Things Are* because my students were familiar with this story but had not yet discussed it in terms of the hero cycle. I think it is better to teach from books students have already encountered because they are not focusing entirely on what will happen next in the story. It is possible that students will design new versions of the hero cycle during their small-group discussions to represent how stories are structured. Cumulative stories, predictable books, counting books, and ABC books all have different structures, and we may try to represent these structures on different charts and diagrams later in the year. This opens up new avenues for discussing story structures and how we can represent them.

FIG. L2.1
The Hero (or Heroine) Cycle

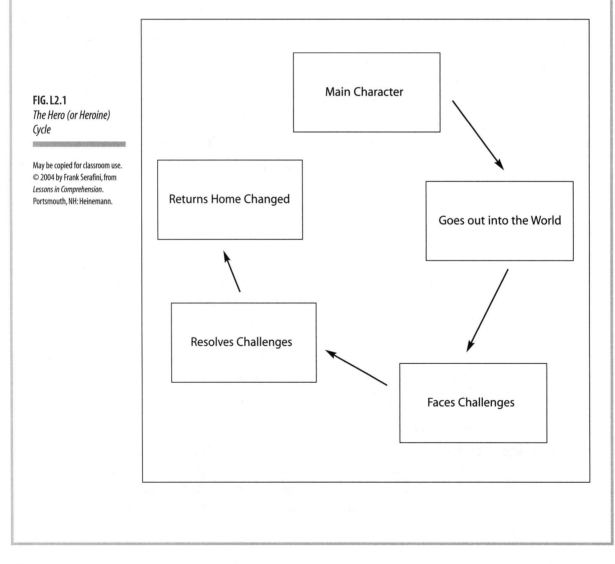

Using Diagrams to Understand Story Structures

The Challenge: Even though novice readers are able to follow along with the plot of a story and discuss the characters and settings of a selection of children's literature, they often have difficulties understanding the overall structure of a story (for example, see The Hero Cycle, Lesson 2.1). Some picture books have structures that are overt, for example, alphabet books, counting books, cumulative stories, pattern books, and predictable books, while the structures of other stories are less recognizable. As the structures of stories become more complex, novice readers need more support in recognizing and understanding the overall structure of the story in order to make sense of what they are reading.

My Intentions: This series of lessons is designed to introduce a variety of diagrams to help readers become aware of a variety of story structures, from simple pattern books to complex novels. It is my contention that helping readers understand the big picture will help them come to more sophisticated understandings of the text, make stronger intertextual connections, and be able to see how individual elements of a story work in harmony to create a piece of literature.

Lesson Overview: In this series of lessons that parallel the use of the hero cycle in Lesson 2.1, I present students with a variety of diagrams, or graphic organizers, based on particular story structures to help novice readers see how we can visually represent these structures. I invite students to make their own diagrams and explain how these diagrams help them understand a story's structure.

How It Might Go: Good morning, Readers! Remember when I showed you that flowchart for the book *Where the Wild Things Are*? Remember we called it the hero cycle and said that it was one type of story structure? Well, there are many kinds of structures for stories, and over the next few days we are going to investigate some diagrams that represent different types of story structures (see Figure L2.2 for examples). Let's look at one I call the bell curve. This diagram represents the action that takes place in a story. When the line is low, like at the beginning of the curved line, there isn't much going on, but then when the line goes up, it's probably a really exciting time in the story. Then, if you look at the diagram, the line goes back down and the story sort of finishes up. Let's read the book *Edward and the Pirates*, by David McPhail (1997), again. Do you remember this story? Well, let's read it again and see if it fits the bell curve structure.

FIG. L2.2
Story Structure Diagrams

May be copied for classroom use.
© 2004 by Frank Serafini, from
Lessons in Comprehension.
Portsmouth, NH: Heinemann.

The Bell Curve

Intensity

Story Episodes / Action

Time Lines

Time

Parallel Story Lines

Guided Practice: After I demonstrate how *Edward and the Pirates* fits the bell curve diagram, I have students in small groups construct their own diagrams of picture books with relatively apparent story structures like the one I call the bell curve. I always demonstrate how a particular diagram relates to a particular story structure before I ask students to make diagrams independently. As we encounter more and more sophisticated texts, we will create new diagrams to represent the overall structures of the stories.

Closing Comments: The purpose of these lessons is not to get good at creating diagrams of story structures! The purpose is to use these representations of story structures to help readers make more sophisticated interpretations and understandings of the texts they read. This is not easy. Young readers have rarely been asked to think about structure, relying instead on individual elements of literature—plot, character, setting—to describe the texts they read. It takes time for students to begin to see stories as a whole and to see how the structure supports the story. I encourage you to develop your own diagrams to represent particular story structures. There is no single formula, just whatever works for you and your students.

Central Tensions and Resolutions

The Challenge: Almost every piece of literature contains tensions or problems characters must face during the course of the story. Often, these tensions are resolved before the end of the story, although sometimes they are left unresolved. It is this central tension that keeps the reader turning the page and students begging teachers to keep reading the story to them. As readers, we just want to find out what happens next in the stories that matter to us. The more readers are able to recognize these tensions and understand how tension adds to a story, the better they will be able to make sense of what they are reading.

My Intentions: This series of lessons is designed to help readers identify tensions in pieces of literature and understand how authors and illustrators use tension to entice the reader through the story.

Lesson Overview: Using a double-entry, or T-chart, I will help novice readers identify and discuss the tensions in a story and how the author chose to resolve each tension, either by offering a solution or leaving it open for the reader to decide. On one side of the chart, we list the challenges the characters face, and on the other side, we note ideas about how they faced them or what they could have done differently. It is not simply a scavenger hunt for the elements of literature in a story; rather, it is a discussion about how the author used these elements to create the story.

How It Might Go: Good morning, Readers! This morning you may have noticed behind me on the classroom wall a new kind of chart. This is called a double-entry chart, or a T-chart because it looks like a *T* (see Figure L2.3). On one side I have written the word *Tensions* and the other side I have written the word *Resolutions*. Could any of you tell me what these two words mean? [Discussion and use of the dictionary.] Good! Tensions are things that are challenging or problems characters face. Resolutions are ways problems or arguments get solved. In our story today, *Dinosaur Bob and His Adventures with the Family Lazardo*, by William Joyce (1995), we are going to see that the Family Lazardo encounters a series of challenges as they try to bring home a dinosaur they discovered on their vacation. Sounds like fun, finding a dinosaur on vacation. As we read the story, if you recognize a challenge for the characters, let's list it on the Tensions side of the chart and then when the story is finished, we will go back and talk about how William Joyce decided to resolve the challenges and if he could've done it differently. Remember, we want to know how these tensions and resolutions affect the story. Okay?

FIG. L2.3
Tensions and Resolutions in Dinosaur Bob and His Adventures with the Family Lazardo

May be copied for classroom use.
© 2004 by Frank Serafini, from
Lessons in Comprehension.
Portsmouth, NH: Heinemann.

Tensions	Resolutions
Should they bring Dinosaur Bob back from their vacation?	Yes, they brought him back.
What will happen when they get Dinosaur Bob back from Africa?	He was stared at by a lot of people. He ended up playing on the Pimlico baseball team.
How will they get Dinosaur Bob out of jail?	They broke him out of jail and hid him on the baseball team.

Guided Practice: After we have done this experience with a few books as a whole group, I will have students try to identify tensions and resolutions in small groups with selected pieces of literature. After that has been successful, I will ask students to discuss tension and resolution in their literature response logs.

Closing Comments: *Tensions* and *resolutions* are more inclusive terms than the traditional *problem* and *solution* or *cause* and *effect*. I have chosen to use the terms *tensions* and *resolutions* because not all stories have a simply stated problem, nor a solution to the challenges the characters face in the story. Trying to reduce the tensions inherent in a piece of literature down to a single problem to be identified devalues the complexity that makes literature great. It is the multiplicity of voices and challenges that makes a piece of literature worth reading. Reducing the complexity of a piece of literature detracts from our goal of helping readers develop more sophisticated responses to the literature they experience. Additionally, not all effects have singular or identifiable causes, and not all problems are solved at the end of the story. Many great pieces of children's literature, Chris Van Allsburg books, for example, leave the resolution of the tension up to the reader.

Interplay Between Text and Illustrations

The Challenge: Teachers and students have begun to learn how to focus on texts and on illustrations, but rarely do they focus on the relationships between the text and the illustrations in children's picture books. There has been some interesting research in the area of visual design and art theory that provides unique insights about this relationship. While it is important to be able to discuss the media used by different artists and the literary devices used by various writers, we also need to provide readers with the language to talk about the relationships between text and illustrations and to call their attention to this aspect of children's picture books.

My Intentions: This series of lessons is designed to introduce readers to three general relationships that have been described in the research literature about the interplay between text and illustrations, namely symmetrical, enhancing, and contradictory relationships.

Lesson Overview: Using examples of children's literature, I will demonstrate the various ways that texts and illustrations are related to each other. Although these relationships often overlap, there are many picture books that provide clear examples of the three general relationships. A symmetrical relationship means that the text and the illustrations provide about the same information, for example the word *ball* and a picture of a ball. Of course, they don't provide exactly the same meanings, but they are symmetrical in content. An enhancing relationship means that the text enhances the story told in the illustrations, and the illustrations enhance the story told in the text. This is the most common relationship in contemporary children's picture books. The third, a contradictory relationship, occurs in many examples of postmodern picture books (see booklist on my website). In this relationship, what happens in the text is contradictory to what is represented in the illustrations. Perry Nodelman, a recognized expert in children's literature, has described this relationship as having a sense of irony. In any case, the illustrations and the text tell a different story.

How It Might Go: Good morning, Readers! Remember when you used to read simple picture books where each page had one word and a picture of what the word was about? I remember *Are You My Mother?* by P. D. Eastman (1960). The pictures went along with the words on every page. Now that we are reading more sophisticated books, have you noticed that some illustrations go along with the story, and sometimes they are different than the story? This is because authors and illustrators create different relationships between the words and the pictures. I call this relationship the *interplay* between texts and illustrations. That's probably a new word for many of you. Interplay is like singing and dancing a song at the same time. Two different things happening at once. Well, the same thing happens in children's picture books. We have the illustrations to look at and the words to read at the same time. When we open to a page, we usually look at the pictures and read the words on that page before going on to the next page. We don't read all the words through the whole book and then go back and look at all the pictures. That would be pretty weird, wouldn't it? I am going to show you some examples of three kinds of relationships that exist in picture books. We will call them symmetrical, enhancing, and contradictory. We will talk about symmetrical relationships, just like we talked about symmetry in geometry. Then we will talk about enhancing relationships, like when someone enhances a picture in art. And then we will talk about contradictory relationships, like when someone disagrees with someone else. Let's put those three words on a chart and see if we can begin to define what each of them means as we go along. Okay?

Guided Practice: Because this may be a very new concept for many students, I take my time discussing each relationship and provide numerous examples before having students look for the relationships in their self-selected picture books.

Closing Comments: This is not an exact science, so to speak. Many picture books exhibit characteristics from each of these categories. The idea is to get students to start looking at the text and the illustrations as interrelated symbol systems, instead of as separate entities.

FIG. L2.4
Symmetrical, Enhancing, and Contradictory Relationships

May be copied for classroom use.
© 2004 by Frank Serafini, from *Lessons in Comprehension.* Portsmouth, NH: Heinemann.

Symmetrical

I'm as Quick as a Cricket, by Audrey Wood

Green Eggs and Ham, by Dr. Seuss

Caps for Sale, by Esphyr Slobodkina

Enhancing

What Are You So Grumpy About? by Tom Lichtenheld

David Goes to School, by David Shannon

Grandfather's Journey, by Allen Say

Officer Buckle and Gloria, by Peggy Rathmann

Contradictory

Just Another Ordinary Day, by Rod Clement

Bamboozled, by David Legge

Changes, by Anthony Browne

The Three Pigs, by David Wiesner

Point of View

The Challenge: In order to understand literature and other texts, readers have to understand that the author uses a character or a narrator to tell the story. In addition, in picture books, illustrators use different points of view in their illustrations to create particular effects. Depending on whose perspective or point of view the story is being told from, readers are privy to particular characters' insights and excluded from others. Readers need to be able to determine who is telling the story and how this affects how the story is told, in both text and illustrations.

My Intentions: This series of lessons is designed to help students investigate the concept of point of view in literature. Being able to describe the perspective from which a story is told enriches the reader's understandings of a piece of literature.

Lesson Overview: Using picture books that have contrasting points of view (see Figure L2.5), we can begin to discuss how perspectives can change how a story is told. I use these picture books to develop perspective in our writing workshop as well. I want students to be able to identify from whose point of view the story is being told, but more importantly, I want readers to be able to discuss how this affects the telling of the story. I want them to understand how the story would be different if another character or narrator told the story.

How It Might Go: Good morning, Readers! Remember when we read the book *Gila Monsters Meet You at the Airport*, by Marjorie Weinman Sharmat (1980)? Let's take another look at that funny story about the boy who was moving from New York to Arizona and the other boy who

FIG. L2.5
Picture Books with Contrasting Points of View

Yo! Yes?, by Chris Rashka

Glasses: Who Needs 'Em? by Lane Smith

The True Story of the Three Little Pigs, by Jon Scieszka

Zoo, by Anthony Browne

Bub, or The Very Best Thing, by Natalie Babbitt

John Patrick Norman McHennessey, by John Burningham

was moving from Arizona to New York. [Read story.] What's going on here? Does anybody notice how each part of the story is different? The first part of the story tells what the boy from New York City thinks about Arizona. Was he right? Then, the second part of the books tells what the boy from Arizona thinks about New York City. Was he right? We call what the author is doing contrasting points of view. The author is trying to tell you that the boy from New York and the one from Arizona have different points of view. In fact, their points of view are distorted. They are wrong about what they think they know or don't understand something because of the experiences they have had in their lives. If I told you that we were moving to Alaska next week, what do you think you would see there? [Students offer ideas about igloos and polar bears and Eskimos.] Let's take a look at a book about Juneau, Alaska. Juneau is the capital of the state of Alaska. From the pictures, it looks like a regular city. Do you think polar bears would meet you at the airport? Let's talk about why we thought the things we did about Alaska and then read the book some more.

Guided Practice: Once students have a sense of what point of view means, I have them look at a series of picture books in small groups and identify from whose point of view each story is being told. Then, we discuss how this affects the story. When this has been successful, I ask students to write in their literature response logs about whose point of view the novel they are reading for homework is written from. I ask them to write about how that point of view affects the story they are reading.

Closing Comments: Before I can introduce terms like *first-person singular* and *narrator*, I need to help readers understand what point of view means. By choosing picture books where the point of view is blatantly apparent, we can begin to understand how it affects the story being told. Authors and illustrators tell stories from particular points of view for a reason; it is not a haphazard guess. First-person point of view gives the reader an intimate portrayal of one person's perspective about the world and the events in a story. When an author uses an outside narrator to tell a story, we get a very different perspective. Third-person narrators tend to give a more balanced or global account of events in the story.

Themes

The Challenge: Like symbols and the use of symbolism (see Lesson 2.7), theme is an abstract concept and one that challenges novice and experienced readers alike. Themes are constructed by readers based on their knowledge of the world and what the author created in the text. I believe that there are multiple themes in most pieces of literature. The discussions that focus on themes should not be conducted to narrow down the possibilities to the one correct theme; rather, our discussions should investigate the multiple possibilities to see what sense readers are making of the text and its connection to their world.

My Intentions: This series of lessons is designed to introduce the concept of theme by relating themes to children's everyday experiences and using that knowledge to understand themes in literature.

Lesson Overview: Using fables, theme parks, anthologies of poetry, parties, restaurant experiences, and other ideas, I will present the concept of theme to my students. The texts and experiences that I will use have themes that are easily recognized or deduced and this knowledge will help readers transfer the concept of theme to the literature we read. I want students to understand abstract concepts like theme, symbols, and mood by referring to their life experiences and the language they use before trying to relate to the literature we are reading.

How It Might Go: Good morning, Readers! Have any of you ever been to a theme park? [Discussion.] What does it mean to be a "theme" park? Let's write the word *theme* here on our chart paper. Could someone look up the word *theme* in the dictionary while we are discussing theme parks? Thanks. Remember when we were reading poetry, we read a lot of anthologies. An anthology is a collection of poetry that is gathered together around a particular idea. Each anthology had what we called a central idea. That is very similar to the idea we are discussing today. [Have several examples of clearly defined poetry anthologies available.] Have any of you ever been to a party that had a theme or a restaurant that had one? [Continued discussion.] Each of these things had what I am going to call a central theme, meaning that everything about the party or amusement park or restaurant focused on or related to one particular idea or topic. In the stories we read there is often an underlying theme that the author is trying to get readers to think about. Unlike theme parks and restaurants, the theme in literature isn't usually directly stated in the story. We have to infer, or construct, what that theme is. I am going to read a book called *Odd Velvet*, by Mary E. Whitcomb (1998). I would like you to think about what possible themes come to your mind when I am reading the book and then we will discuss our ideas. Ready?

Guided Practice: Because the concept of theme is an abstract one, I would support novice readers' discussions about theme for a long period before sending them out to construct themes from more complex materials on their own. I would begin in small groups with fables or picture books where the themes are fairly obvious and then use fairy tales, which is a genre that my students were familiar with, to discuss the theme of good versus evil, for example.

Closing Comments: Themes are a difficult concept to grasp. One of the most important understandings that I want students to take away from this series of lessons is the idea that literature relates to the world and that there are meanings that go beyond the boundaries of the story itself. I want students to understand that literature relates to, and illuminates, life. The themes that we are constructing are relationships between a story and the world in which we live.

FIG. L2.6
Picture Books with Readily Available Themes

May be copied for classroom use.
© 2004 by Frank Serafini, from *Lessons in Comprehension.*
Portsmouth, NH: Heinemann.

Tacky the Penguin, by Helen Lester

Sister Anne's Hands, by Mary Beth Lorbiecki

The Recess Queen, by Alexis O'Neill

Horace and Morris, but Mostly Dolores, by James Howe

Elmer, by David McKee

This Is Our House, by Michael Rosen

Metropolitan Cow, by Tim Egan

Lily's Purple Plastic Purse, by Kevin Henkes

Koala Lou, by Mem Fox

Symbols and Symbolism

The Challenge: Symbols are abstract concepts that require a great deal of background knowledge in order to understand the connections authors make to ideas in the world outside of texts. Novice readers often miss these symbols in literature, not because of their reading abilities per se, but rather because of their lack of worldly experiences. By beginning with concrete examples of symbols that have readily identifiable relationships with things or ideas in the world, for example, product logos, we can help readers understand the idea of symbolic relationships and then make connections to how these relationships are used in literature and poetry.

My Intentions: This series of lessons is designed to help readers understand the concept of a symbol and how symbols are used in children's literature and poetry. Symbols are abstract relationships among items in a story and things or concepts in the world. Understanding these relationships is not easy and requires a lot of support and guidance.

Lesson Overview: Beginning with product logos, especially those from sportswear, cars, and sports teams, I attempt to get students to understand the relationship between a logo or symbol and its product. For example, Mercury, the god of speed, is used for FTD florists to represent fast delivery. Once the concept of a symbol is understood, I use traditional fairy tales to demonstrate the use of symbols, in particular good versus evil as symbolized by pigs and wolves.

How It Might Go: Good morning, Readers! Today we are going to talk about symbols. No, not the ones you bang on in the orchestra. As I look around, I notice that a lot of you are wearing shirts or shorts that have little marks or figures on them. These symbols are called logos. They are used to help people recognize the type of sportswear you are wearing. Let's make a list of some of these on the board. [Discussion.] In literature, authors and illustrators often use symbols to represent other things, like good or evil or important things in our lives. For example, we have read many different versions of fairy tales, in particular the Three Little Pigs stories. In most of the versions, the wolf is the bad guy, isn't he? We could say that the wolf is a symbol for evil or the bad guy. Are there any other stories or fairy tales you can think of where the wolf is used as a symbol of evil or the bad guy? [Discussion. See booklist on website.] In each of the stories we have just listed, who is usually the good guy? That's right, the pigs. So, the pig can be thought of as a symbol for the good guy. Now, in *Three Little Wolves and the Big Bad Pig,* by Eugene Trivizas (1997), the author has reversed the roles so that the pig is bad and the wolves are good. Let's see if we can find other examples of symbols in some of the fairy tales we have read [see website for list of fairy tales from a different point of view].

Guided Practice: I assign students in small groups to review other versions of fairy tales, both traditional and fractured, to see who represents good and evil. We come back together and discuss the use of symbols in fairy tales.

Closing Comments: Before students can identify and understand the symbols in more complex poetry and literature, they need to understand what symbols are and how the symbolic relationships are used in the stories they read. By starting our discussions with symbols that children encounter in their everyday lives, we can help them recognize and understand the symbols used in literature.

FIG. L2.7
Picture Books with Easily Recognizable Symbols

The Rabbits, by John Marsden

The Big Orange Splot, by Daniel Pinkwater

Feathers and Fools, by Mem Fox

The Straight Line Wonder, by Mem Fox

The Big Box, by Toni and Slade Morrison

White Socks Only, by Evelyn Coleman

Mood

The Challenge: Mood is something that we recognize but probably don't pay much conscious attention to in literature or film, especially if it has been well constructed. When we go to a horror film or read a scary story, we don't think about why it takes place on a stormy night in an old house; we almost come to expect it. Mood plays an important role in helping readers make an emotional connection to the stories they read. It adds to the tension of a story and creates expectations in the reader's mind by relating to his previous experiences.

My Intentions: This series of lessons is designed to help bring the concept of mood to readers' conscious attention. When readers begin to notice how authors and illustrators create the mood of a story through language and illustrations, they will understand the story more completely and may begin to use these devices in their writing.

Lesson Overview: I draw on two picture books with contrasting moods to help readers recognize mood in literature and discuss the elements the authors and illustrators used to create those moods.

How It Might Go: Good morning, Readers! Have you ever been to a scary movie? Where or when do these stories usually take place? [Discussion.] Why do they take place in creepy old houses or graveyards? [Discussion.] Today we are going to take a look at two picture books that are very different. The first one is called *Night of the Gargoyles*, by Eve Bunting (1999), and the second is called *Officer Buckle and Gloria*, by Peggy Rathmann (1995). Let's take a look at the two covers. One book is illustrated in black and white and the other one is drawn in bright colors. Just looking at the covers and reading the titles, what do you notice about these two books? Let me read some parts of each book to you and let's see if you notice anything different about the way each book has been written. Then, we will look at the kinds of illustrations in each book and discuss what the illustrations suggest. [Read and discuss books.] One of the differences in these two books is what we call the mood. When we say that someone is in a good or bad mood, what do we mean? Is there a connection between being in a certain mood and creating a mood in a story? Let's talk about this for awhile.

Guided Practice: Like the last two series of lessons focusing on symbols and themes, mood is an abstract concept, but one that has more connection to readers and is more readily recognized than the other two. I would support our initial discussions with small-group discussions and with individual responses in literature logs.

Closing Comments: Like symbols and themes, I introduce mood through reading aloud particular picture books and focusing on important points I want to attend to. The purpose is to bring to conscious attention particular aspects of literature to help readers come to more sophisticated responses to their readings. Terms like *mood*, *theme*, and *symbol* have to become part of the language used in our reading workshop. The idea is to use these terms in our discussions, not to quiz students on their vocabulary understandings.

FIG. L2.8
Picture Books with Easily Recognizable Moods

Nettie's Trip South, by Ann Turner

Click, Clack, Moo, by Doreen Cronin

Owl Moon, by Jane Yolen

The Bus Ride, by William Miller

Mean Soup, by Betsy Everitt

Navigating Text

*D*ecoding is narrowly defined as the ability to break the code of written language or, more commonly, learning how to sound out letters and words. Decoding focuses primarily on letter-sound relationships and often ignores other linguistic and textual knowledge readers use to make sense of the texts they read. In addition to learning decoding strategies, readers need to be able to understand design elements, directionality, illustrations, and story structures. As readers progress into more complicated texts, decoding becomes part of a larger process I am describing as navigating text.

Literary devices, like foreshadowing and flashback, the use of unusual fonts, nonlinear story structures, and unique textual elements, present readers with new challenges. In addition to the traditional cognitive-based comprehension strategies and decoding strategies, these lessons are designed to help readers navigate picture books and other contemporary reading materials. Helping novice readers approach texts in new and different ways is the intention of each of the lessons included in this strand.

During a time when teachers are being asked to hurry up and cover more in the curriculum, I believe we have lost the depth of thinking required to construct meaning from many of the texts we encounter. I am suggesting that we slow down and attend to the variety of elements, literary devices, and possible meanings that are generated with the complex examples of children's literature available today. We can only learn so much from a book that we have read once. Quality literature does not reveal itself in a single pass. Helping readers navigate these pieces of literature is crucial if we are going to develop successful readers in our schools.

The comprehension lessons in this section include:

1. Reading Strategies Bookmarks

2. Investigating Fonts and Visual Design Elements

3. Approaching a Text

4. Rules of Notice

5. Attending to Punctuation

6. Reading Wordless Picture Books

7. Previewing a Text

8. Reading Postmodern Picture Books

Reading Strategies Bookmarks

The Challenge: Novice readers often rely on two primary reading strategies: sounding words out and asking someone for help. Research shows us that successful readers have a repertoire of reading strategies they can draw upon when confronted with difficult texts. Readers need to be able to use a variety of strategies when they are reading to understand what they read and help them become self-monitoring, independent, successful readers.

My Intentions: I want to introduce novice readers to a variety of authentic reading strategies, strategies that readers actually use when they are reading texts. If readers are able to recognize the strategies they already use and can be introduced to several new strategies within the context of an actual reading event, they will be more likely to see the purpose for these strategies and begin to use them independently.

Lesson Overview: Using a collaborative cloze procedure with a repetitive, predictable story in big-book format, students generate a list of reading strategies they use to make sense of texts. As we create this list, we make bookmarks with the strategies listed on them for students to use while they are reading to remind them of the strategies we have discussed.

How It Might Go: Good morning, Reading Researchers! That's right, reading researchers. Today, we are going to investigate what we do when we are reading a book to see what strategies we use to make sense of stories. We are going to slow down and think about what we do when we are reading through a text. I have a big book we are going to read, called *Is Your Mama a Llama?* by Deborah Guarino (1997). It's a funny story about a little llama searching for his mama. As we begin to read through this book together, you will see that there are words that I have covered up with Post-its. When I come to one of those words when I am reading, I am going to substitute the word *blank* in its place. After I finish reading the page, I am going to ask you to quietly raise your hand if you think you know what the covered-up word is. Please don't yell out the word, so that other students can think for themselves. If I call on you to tell me what the word is, please be ready to tell me your prediction *and* what you did to figure it out. That's what we are interested in: how you figured it out. We are going to make a chart listing all the things we do, called reading strategies, to make sense of the story. Okay? I will start reading and you will be on the lookout for those words that are covered up.

Guided Practice: When our reading strategies bookmarks are completed, I make sure that readers use the bookmarks when they are doing independent and paired reading. I want the strategies to become automatic. I reinforce these strategies during guided reading groups and one-on-one student reading conferences.

Closing Comments: During the cloze procedure, it is important to keep the discussion about the strategies and not about who guesses correctly. I purposefully choose words that require readers to use specific strategies and context clues. Some of the words I cover up are easy to guess, while others have more than one possible answer. It is most important that readers make guesses that are plausible, not necessarily correct. I explain that authors have many choices of words when they are writing a book, and it is important that the guesses we make are logical and make sense, but they don't necessarily have to be the exact word the author chose.

The first and foremost strategy that readers need to understand is that reading is about making meaning or sense of a text. Without this as the primary strategy or purpose for reading, readers would never know when to employ any of the other strategies. As experienced readers, we monitor for meaning and use a strategy or reread a passage when meaning breaks down. Like so many of the tools in this book, we need to keep in mind that reading strategies are used in the *service of meaning,* not as an end in themselves.

FIG. L3.1
Reading Strategies Bookmark

May be copied for classroom use.
© 2004 by Frank Serafini, from *Lessons in Comprehension.*
Portsmouth, NH: Heinemann.

Our Reading Strategies

- ❖ Ask yourself:
  1. Does it make sense?
  2. Does it sound right?
  3. Does it look right?
- ❖ Reread parts that are confusing.
- ❖ Think about what you know.
- ❖ Read ahead and go back.
- ❖ Look at the punctuation.
- ❖ *Think.*
- ❖ Sound it out.
- ❖ Look at the pictures.
- ❖ Look for words in words.
- ❖ Stop and ask yourself what the story is about.
- ❖ Make connections.
- ❖ Ask questions.

Investigating Fonts and Visual Design Elements

The Challenge: The fonts used in picture books and how text is displayed across the pages can often confuse novice readers. If readers are not sure where the text goes next, it's hard to follow along and make sense of it. Readers need to learn to navigate through a selection, following the text, recognizing various fonts and other design elements, and using extratextual material to comprehend what they are reading.

My Intentions: This series of lessons is designed to help students recognize the variety of fonts used in children's literature and develop strategies for navigating unusual textual design structures.

Lesson Overview: Using a variety of texts that employ unusual fonts and design elements (magazines, newspapers, brochures, greeting cards, and selected picture books), I present groupings of letters and discuss how we can recognize these when we are reading. By helping readers draw upon syntactical cues, semantic cues, and context clues, I am able to help readers monitor what they are reading and employ strategies for navigating texts.

How It Might Go: Good morning, Readers! You will see behind me on the wall a series of letters. Let's look closely at what I have out up there. [Look at twenty different versions of the letters F and S.] That's right, those are my initials. Every one of those says the exact same thing. Look at how many different varieties of letters there are. I took these from different books, magazines, and newspapers. How can we recognize these letters when we see them in the books we read? [Discussion of strategies.] If we rely on only sounding it out, then it may get more confusing. We have to recognize the context of the words as well as the words themselves.

I am going to share with you a pile of books that I think might present some challenges to you because of the fonts that are used and the way the publisher designed the text. In small groups, we are going to read through one book each and generate a few suggestions for each other about how you made sense of the fonts, the text, and the design. Keep track of your strategies and be ready to share them with the whole class when I call you back together.

Guided Practice: While students are working through these texts in small groups, I circulate, take notes, and offer suggestions. I believe that having students work as reading detectives, making reading an inquiry process, helps them become strategic, self-monitoring readers. I try to use small groups to bring to conscious awareness the strategies we use when we read. These strategies are then reinforced throughout our reading workshop.

Closing Comments: Many readers have no problem recognizing unusual fonts. In general, these readers employ many strategies when reading. However, readers that rely exclusively on graphophonic cues often have trouble making sense of new fonts and irregular design elements. Readers need to take into account the full range of cues available and become comfortable with a variety of fonts and textual designs.

FIG. L3.2
Picture Books That Contain Challenging Design Elements

May be copied for classroom use. © 2004 by Frank Serafini, from *Lessons in Comprehension*. Portsmouth, NH: Heinemann.

The Frog Who Wanted to Be a Singer, by Linda Goss

The Watertower, by Gary Crew

Horace and Morris, but Mostly Dolores, by James Howe

The Eleventh Hour, by Graeme Base

The Straight Line Wonder, by Mem Fox

Starry Messenger, by Peter Sis

The Three Pigs, by David Wiesner

The Jolly Postman, by Allan and Janet Ahlberg

The Discovery of Dragons, by Graeme Base

How Dogs Really Work, by Alan Snow

The Secret Knowledge of Grown-Ups, by David Wisniewski

Approaching a Text

The Challenge: Novice readers tend to pick up a new chapter or picture book and turn past the front matter to the first page of text and start reading. In contemporary picture books, and a growing number of chapter books, many clues are embedded in the dedication, dust jacket, author's notes, and other front matter. Readers need to attend to this material in order to make sense of contemporary children's literature.

My Intentions: This series of lessons is designed to call students' attention to the wealth of information and clues to the story that can often be found in the front matter of a text. I want to demonstrate to students how I approach a text, what I do before I begin reading, and the things I attend to that add to my understanding and enjoyment of the story.

Lesson Overview: Using a variety of picture books that contain extensive amounts of information and clues in the extratextual and front matter, I will demonstrate to students how I approach a text.

How It Might Go: Good morning, Reading Detectives! That's right, reading detectives! In many ways, reading is like being a detective, searching for clues and trying to understand what is happening in a text. When you choose a book to read and start reading, what do you do? [Discussion.] I hope you don't just turn to the first page and start reading. A reading detective would not do that! In many of the picture books that we have been reading, you might have been lost if you didn't look at the dedication, title pages, and author's notes before reading the text. Let's take a look at the book *The Stinky Cheese Man and Other Fairly Stupid Tales,* by Jon Scieszka (1993). On the back cover is a chicken yelling about the ISBN number. Did you notice that? If you look at the dust jacket, you will notice that the author and illustrator pictures are of George Washington and Abraham Lincoln, off the one- and five-dollar bills. Why do you think they did that? There are a bunch of jokes on the opening dust jacket as well. If you just opened the book and started reading, you would have missed all of that. Let me show you what I do when I pick up a new picture book. [Model studying the front matter of a book.]

Guided Practice: The language describing the various parts of picture books needs to become part of our normal classroom discussions. We should use and reinforce terms like *dust jacket* and *front matter* throughout our discussions. I often ask students to include the elements of literature and parts of a picture book in their literature response logs. These terms are used in our guided reading groups and strategy lessons as well.

Closing Comments: I demonstrate how I approach a text by thinking aloud in front of my students as I read a picture book. I say out loud what is going on in my head, what I am looking at, and what I am thinking. I want students to slow down and attend to all the parts of the book. It is a calling to conscious attention the elements of a text that many students take for granted.

FIG. L3.3
Picture Books with Extensive Extratextual Material

The Stinky Cheese Man and Other Fairly Stupid Tales, by Jon Scieszka

Black and White, by David Macauley

The Discovery of Dragons, by Graeme Base

Tibet, by Peter Sis

Snowflake Bentley, by Jacqueline Briggs Martin

So You Want to Be President?, by Judith St. George

Table Manners, by Chris Raschka

Willy's Pictures, by Anthony Browne

Rules of Notice

The Challenge: All visual elements of a piece of literature (text, images, illustrations, headings, chapter titles, epigraphs) do not provide the same amount of information to the reader. Peter Rabinowitz, a prominent literary theorist, has described four rules that readers need to understand to make sense of literature. One of those rules is called the Rule of Notice. He suggests that certain words, and other visual elements of a text, are privileged over others, meaning readers should attend to them more than other elements when making sense of a text. Novice readers often assign equal attention to all elements of a text. We need to help readers understand how we dedicate our attention to particular elements in a text over other elements.

My Intentions: By thinking aloud during a whole-group read-aloud, I intend to demonstrate to readers what elements of a text deserve more attention than others.

Lesson Overview: This series of lessons is designed to demonstrate how I focus my attention on particular elements as I read a text. Using complex picture books that contain a vast array of visual and textual elements, I will demonstrate what features I attend to and why I feel they are important for making meaning while I am reading.

How It Might Go: Good morning, Readers! When you are reading a picture book, have you ever noticed that you spend more time looking at certain images and reading certain words than others? I certainly do. I pay close attention to things like the chapter titles, if there are any, and the illustrations at the beginning of the book. When I am reading a nonfiction or expository text, I pay close attention to subheadings and captions because I know I can learn a lot by attending to those elements. I guess what I am saying is that not all parts of a book are created equal, and some deserve more attention than others. Let me show you what I mean. I am going to read the book *Santa Calls*, by William Joyce (2001), to you today. I want to show you that I pay close attention to some aspects of the book and just glance at others. What I pay the most attention to depends on what my purpose for reading the book is. Let's take a look at the book. The first thing I notice is that there are small pictures hidden in the title page and dedication pages. Since I already know that this is a mystery-adventure book because I read a review of the book before I bought it, I know that I have to pay close attention to the details in order to solve the mystery. Remember when we read *The Eleventh Hour*, by Graeme Base (1989), there were all those clues hidden in the illustrations? Well, maybe William Joyce hid some clues in these illustrations as well. Also, I am thinking about the title of the book, *Santa Calls*. What does that mean, he calls? Whom does he call? Let's begin reading this book and as I am reading, stop me if you think what you see or hear might be a clue to solving the mystery. Let's read through this book slowly and talk about what we are attending to.

Guided Practice: As we begin helping readers slow down and approach a text differently, we need to support these practices throughout the reading workshop. By creating a chart on how to approach a text, including some rules of notice, we can support readers during their independent and paired reading. One way I do this is by allowing my students to practice in pairs the ideas I demonstrate in my reading lessons. In this example, I would give students some books with a mystery to be solved and they would work in pairs to figure out clues. We would then gather together at the end of the workshop and discuss what worked and what didn't. Helping them attend to books with new eyes is what reading instruction is all about.

Closing Comments: This is certainly not an exact science. Every reader attends to different things for different purposes. However, when we become familiar with a particular genre—mysteries, for example—we learn to attend to particular elements of the story in more detail. I want readers to learn to pay close attention to particular items in a text based on their previous experiences with that kind of story.

FIG. L3.4
Books with a Mystery to Be Solved

May be copied for classroom use.
© 2004 by Frank Serafini, from *Lessons in Comprehension*. Portsmouth, NH: Heinemann.

Santa Calls, by William Joyce

Piggins, by Jane Yolen

Picnic with Piggins, by Jane Yolen

The Stranger, by Chris Van Allsburg

June 29, 1999, by David Wiesner

Grandpa's Teeth, by Rod Clement

Seven Blind Mice, by Ed Young

Bub, or, The Very Best Thing, by Natalie Babbitt

The Eleventh Hour, by Graeme Base

Attending to Punctuation

The Challenge: Punctuation gives the reader clues as to how a text is to be read and can affect the meaning of a text. Many novice readers read through a text in a monotonous tone, sometimes indicating that they are not attending to the punctuation marks or the syntax of a text. Not all parts of a text are meant to be read the same way, with the same emphasis. Helping readers attend to the punctuation of a text helps them make sense and read aloud more fluently.

My Intentions: Using several picture books that rely heavily on punctuation for understanding the story, I will demonstrate how I read aloud and why I read in certain voices and inflections.

Lesson Overview: Using the picture book *Yo! Yes?* by Chris Raschka (1993), I read the story, emphasizing the tone of voice suggested by the punctuation. I overdramatize the punctuation to demonstrate how I would read the selection. This short text, containing thirty-six words including the title, provides an excellent opportunity to demonstrate how punctuation affects the meaning of a story and how it should be read.

How It Might Go: Good morning, Readers! We have talked about punctuation a lot in our writing workshop. We discussed things like commas, periods, question marks, and exclamation points. Why do we use punctuation in our writing? That's right, so the reader will know how you want her to read what you have written. We use punctuation as a set of clues that tell the reader when to pause and when to change his voice for a question. Because writers use different punctuation marks, readers need to pay close attention to those marks when they are reading as well. Today, I would like you to listen carefully as I read the story *Yo! Yes?* by Chris Raschka, to you. Let's take a look at the cover and the title. How would you read the title, paying close attention to the punctuation marks? [Discussion.] I am going to read this story slowly and we can discuss how I read each page and why you think I read it that way. Okay?

Guided Practice: Supporting readers as they dramatize a story or read aloud helps them attend to the punctuation of a text. As readers become more accustomed to attending to the punctuation, they become more accomplished oral readers.

Closing Comments: Of course, all texts use punctuation. However, texts like *Yo! Yes?* offer readers the opportunity to attend to the punctuation in order to read the story with emotion and understanding.

Reading Wordless Picture Books

The Challenge: Wordless picture books are an underused resource in the elementary classroom. Teachers are often reluctant to read these books aloud because of the lack of words and the limited role the teacher plays when reading aloud a wordless picture book. I believe they feel uncomfortable sitting there simply turning pages. However, wordless picture books provide opportunities for readers to focus entirely on the visual images to make sense of the story.

My Intentions: Using relatively complex wordless picture books, I demonstrate how a reader navigates through the story. I want novice readers to be able to use the images to construct a logical story line and discuss the possibilities the images offer the reader.

Lesson Overview: After making color copies of three complex picture books, I lay the pages of each book across the wall in storyboard fashion. We discuss how to navigate through the images and discuss possible meanings of the text.

How It Might Go: Good morning, Readers! Remember when we put the illustrations from the books *Where the Wild Things Are* and *Voices in the Park* up on the wall of our room so we could see the books from a new perspective? Well, we are going to do that with a couple more books this week. The only difference this time is that the three books we are going to do this with don't have any words in them. That's right, they are wordless picture books. Have any of you ever read any of these? Usually people think these are easy readers, but the ones that I have chosen are actually quite complicated. The three books we will be reading are *Sector 7*, by David Wiesner (1999), *Flying Jake*, by Lane Smith (1988), and *The Snowman*, by Raymond Briggs (1999). How do we read these books if there aren't any words to tell us which way to go or what to pay attention to? Let's list some ideas.

Guided Practice: I have always enjoyed reading wordless picture books myself. I have quite a few in my collection and use them to help students attend to images and illustrations to make meaning with texts. These are always available for my students during reading workshop and I invite students to read and discuss these whenever they like. They provide excellent opportunities for students who struggle with decoding and need help keeping meaning throughout a complete text.

Closing Comments: Wordless picture books should be made available in all intermediate classrooms. These texts help readers deal with directionality and other aspects of navigating a text.

FIG. L3.6
Favorite Wordless Picture Books

May be copied for classroom use.
© 2004 by Frank Serafini, from
Lessons in Comprehension.
Portsmouth, NH: Heinemann.

Anno's Journey, by Mitsumasa Anno

Pancakes for Breakfast, by Tomie dePaola

Tuesday, by David Wiesner (almost wordless)

The Snowman, by Raymond Briggs

Sector 7, by David Wiesner

Flying Jake, by Lane Smith

Previewing a Text

The Challenge: As I have mentioned previously in the Approaching a Text lesson, readers often grab a book, turn to the first page of text, and start reading. In addition to attending to the front matter or peritext, readers would also be supported by previewing the structures, images, and layout of a book before beginning to read.

My Intentions: Primary-grade teachers will often do a picture walk with a book during a guided reading group. This entails having young readers preview the illustrations and make predictions about what they think the story is about before reading. This series of lessons takes intermediate-grade readers through a similar procedure. Previewing a text is intended to activate prior knowledge and get a sense of what to expect throughout the book.

Lesson Overview: Using some new picture books that I am sure most of my students have not seen, I demonstrate how to walk through a text and get a sense of what is involved in the text before I begin reading. The idea is to get readers to *anticipate* what will happen, not necessarily *predict* what will happen.

How It Might Go: Good morning, Readers! We have been discussing how to approach a text, how to pay attention to punctuation, how to look at all of the information that is in the front matter, and what things we should pay attention to. The lesson we are doing today is designed to help you put all of these ideas together to anticipate what will happen in a text *before* we begin reading. Maybe some of you have done something called a picture walk before? Well, it's something like that. We are going to preview a text, looking through the table of contents, skimming through the text, checking out the illustrations and the structure of the book before we read. Let me show you what I mean. I have a new book called [whatever is new when you read this lesson]. I am going to look at the front and back covers, look at the front matter, read the author's note or biographical notes if there are any, and flip through the pages. I am trying to get an idea about what is in this book, so that when I start reading I will have an idea where it is headed.

Guided Practice: With all of the navigation and comprehension strategies or practices that we demonstrate to our students, we need to provide opportunities for readers to try these with the support of more knowledgeable readers, primarily teachers and other students. My reading workshop provides the time and opportunities for readers to practice these strategies and practices in a supportive community of readers. I have students sit in pairs or small groups and preview new picture books that I have selected for them. I invite them to go through the same processes that I demonstrated and discuss how these worked for them. We generally get back together at the end of the workshop to share our ideas and try new ones.

Closing Comments: The difference between predicting and anticipating is that predicting means you are making a guess about what will happen—in other words, you can be right or wrong, depending on what happens in the book. Anticipating means the reader is paying attention to what is happening in the story and thinking about what might logically happen next. This difference may be negligible, but I think it is worth mentioning. When teachers have students make predictions, it often leads to a contest to see who can get it right. This is not productive. Authors have many ways they could've finished a story. When discussing the idea of anticipating, I want readers to discuss what could happen based on what we know about the characters and the story so far. This seems to lead to possibilities, not contests.

Reading Postmodern Picture Books

The Challenge: Contemporary picture books, and some chapter books as well, contain literary elements that can best be described as postmodern. These books contain nonlinear story structures, often having more than one narrator or perspective; self-referential elements, meaning they refer to themselves as books, calling the reader's attention to the fact she is reading a picture book; and the inclusion of surrealistic images or the juxtaposition of unrelated images. These postmodern elements present unique challenges to novice and experienced readers alike.

My Intentions: By calling students' attention to the numerous examples of postmodern literary devices in contemporary picture books, I hope to support novice readers as they encounter these elements in the stories they choose to read.

Lesson Overview: Using the techniques of disrupting a text (see Lesson 4.2) and attending to the front matter and peritext, along with discussions of postmodern literary elements, I will discuss with students how to approach these unique examples of children's literature.

How It Might Go: Good morning, Readers! Have any of you noticed that I have some weird books in my collection? I'm sure you have. Some of the books that I have bought in the past few years are quite different from stories that have a beginning, a middle, and an end. These books I will call postmodern picture books. *Postmodernism* means that the authors and illustrators have broken away from traditional conventions to attract the reader's attention. These books have different perspectives and often don't tell you what happens in the end of the story. Let's take a look at the new Caldecott-winning book *The Three Pigs*, by David Wiesner (2001), and you will see what I am talking about. The story starts out okay, but then the pigs get blown out of the illustrations and into the white space of the book. Here, in one scene, the pig is looking directly at the reader and saying that someone is out there. This is what we call self-referentiality. What that means is the author wants us to know that we are reading a book and that it exists in a different reality. I know that sounds confusing, but let's continue looking at this book and we will talk about it for awhile. What I want you to be able to do is keep your mind open to new possibilities and not try to figure what the book is about too quickly. As readers of postmodern books, we need to be able to entertain ambiguity in order to see the possibilities of these texts. Let's continue.

Guided Practice: The elements of these books may be so new and overwhelming that many readers shut down when the books don't make complete sense after the first reading. It is important that readers learn to revisit a text and explore new possible meanings. For this reason, we will spend time in the reading workshop revisiting old favorites and discussing these books weeks later to see if new ideas arise. In our rush to introduce readers to new texts, we inadvertently model for them a read-it-once-and-move-on mentality. Time in the reading workshop should be spent digging deeper into books we have read once, as well as investigating new ones.

Closing Comments: One of the characteristics of a successful, experienced reader that I try to develop in my students is the ability to suspend closure while they are reading (see Lesson 5.6). What I mean by this is one's ability to hold several meanings as possible without trying to narrow ideas down to a single, main idea. I described this characteristic earlier as the ability to entertain ambiguity. That is a good way of looking at it. Many novice readers

FIG. L3.8
Favorite Postmodern Picture Books

May be copied for classroom use.
© 2004 by Frank Serafini, from
Lessons in Comprehension.
Portsmouth, NH: Heinemann.

The Jolly Postman, by Allan and Janet Ahlberg

The Discovery of Dragons, by Graeme Base

Changes, by Anthony Browne

Voices in the Park, by Anthony Browne

Willy's Pictures, by Anthony Browne

Zoo, by Anthony Browne

Why the Chicken Crossed the Road, by David Macauley

Black and White, by David Macauley

Shortcut, by David Macauley

Home of the Brave, by Allen Say

Stranger in the Mirror, by Allen Say

The Stinky Cheese Man and Other Fairly Stupid Tales, by Jon Scieszka

Starry Messenger, by Peter Sis

Looking for Atlantis, by Colin Thompson

Bad Day at Riverbend, by Chris Van Allsburg

The Three Pigs, by David Wiesner

Tuesday, by David Wiesner

Pish, Posh, Said Hieronymus Bosch, by Nancy Willard

Bright and Early Thursday Evening, by Audrey Wood

approach a new text and expect it to make sense on the first read-through; if it doesn't, they often abandon their reading. As the texts readers choose to read become more complex, the way they approach a text has to change. These books do not reveal themselves during the first reading and require thoughtful attention during several readings for the reader to make sense of what is being read.

Promoting Invested Literature Discussions

One of our primary responsibilities as teachers of literature is to help novice readers interpret literature in more sophisticated and insightful ways. In other words, we are trying to help children talk about books beyond the "I like it!" level. As Ralph Peterson (1992) has suggested, we are trying to support children as they move from conversation to dialogue and critique in their literature discussions. I have used the word *invested discussions* to refer to these sophisticated, insightful discussions.

The invested discussion strategies in this section are intended to expand students' perspectives and extend the ways readers analyze and connect with literature. As a classroom teacher, it is my role to promote discussions about the texts we read and help children deepen their understandings through discussion with other readers. These invested discussion strategies should not become an end in themselves: rather, they are intended as vehicles for expanding literature discussions. The goal is not to get good at graffiti boards, for example; the goal is to be able to have a sophisticated conversation about a text and be willing and able to generate and negotiate meaning with other readers.

The comprehension lessons in this section include:

1. Think, Pair, and Share
2. Disrupting a Text
3. Illustrated Quotes
4. Word Storms
5. Graffiti Boards
6. Walking Journals
7. The Literary Talk Show
8. Readers' Theatre

Think, Pair, and Share

The Challenge: Too often, classroom discussions about literature focus on the teacher and his/her role in the discussion. Teachers ask questions, students respond, and teachers then evaluate students' responses. This has come to be known as the classic initiate-respond-evaluate classroom interaction. In invested literary discussions, we teach students to respond to each other, not simply answer questions posed by the teacher. The challenge is to help students listen to each other and respond appropriately, be willing to generate ideas and meaning with the books being discussed, and negotiate understandings with other members of their community of readers.

My Intentions: Early in the school year, I invite children to turn to another student, share an idea, and listen to the other student's ideas. After students share ideas with each other, I invite them to share their ideas with the whole class. As part of this process, I work with students to conduct discussions without being required to raise their hands. This takes time but drastically changes the nature of our literary discussions.

Lesson Overview: After I read aloud a favorite picture book, students turn to their reading discussion partners and share their ideas. They listen to their partners' ideas and use this brief discussion as a prompt for a large-group discussion.

How It Might Go: Good morning, Readers! You may have noticed that every morning we begin our day, and our reading workshop, by reading a picture book together, and we end every day by sharing part of a chapter book. Today, we are going to try a new discussion strategy called Turn, Pair, and Share. What I would like you to do is select a discussion partner, anyone that you feel you can work well with and not play around, and sit next to him or her as I read this book. As long as you are able to work well together, you will be able to keep your partner. If you choose to play around, I will select a new partner for you or have you share with me. When we have finished sharing our book, we will turn to our partners and share some ideas with them. Listening to your partner is an important thing to do if you want this to work well. Let's give it a try.

Guided Practice: Being able to listen to and share ideas takes time. Students need the opportunity to discuss texts with each other and share ideas with the teacher. The first few times we do this activity, students take extra time to turn and share and are often unsure about what to say. Over time, novice readers learn to share their ideas with each other and ask quality questions of their partners. Eventually, the goal is to help students learn how to enter a conversation without raising hands, be able to listen to each other, and be willing to offer ideas for the whole group to explore.

Closing Comments: I am trying to get myself out of the center of our literature discussions. I want students to be able to share ideas with each other and not just direct all of the talk at me. This is very challenging for students and teachers alike. We have been trained to direct discussions, ask questions, and evaluate students' ideas. It takes time and practice to learn how to politely enter a conversation, listen to others, and engage in dialogue about literature. We talk about the things that help us be part of these conversations and what hinders our discussions. By changing the expectations I have for students and our discussions, I am trying to change the nature of students' thinking about literature. This is not easy.

Disrupting a Text

The Challenge: In order to help readers develop more sophisticated understandings and interpretations of a picture book, we need to help them bring a variety of perspectives with which to analyze the books we read and share. Novice readers often focus on the illustrations in a picture book rather than the text. We want students to understand the interplay between text and illustrations (see Lesson 2.4) as well as the meanings associated with each separately.

My Intentions: By presenting the illustrations in storyboard fashion, the text typed on a single sheet (disrupting the text), and as a complete picture book, I force students to analyze the elements of the text in new ways.

Lesson Overview: Using select picture books, this series of lessons is designed to help novice readers experience a picture book from a variety of perspectives. First, we read and discuss the selected picture book over a few days, making discussion charts and other response artifacts (see Strand 7). Second, I make color copies of the illustrations of the selected picture book and hang them on the wall in storyboard fashion. Then, I type the text on a single sheet of paper to show the structure of the text and the language used. Finally, we read the complete picture book again and discuss it.

How It Might Go: Good morning, Readers! We have been reading and discussing the book *Voices in the Park*, by Anthony Browne (1998), for the past few days. We have noticed many new things by reading through it a few times. Well, today you have probably noticed the illustrations of the book are hanging behind me on the wall. I have hung them in four rows to represent the four voices in the book. We are going to talk about the illustrations for a couple of days and then we will look at the text without the illustrations to see what else we can notice.

Guided Practice: The object of these lessons is to help readers see picture books from a variety of perspectives. As reading time occurs each day, I use the discussions and the experiences from our whole-group lessons to support the conversations I have with individual readers.

Closing Comments: I don't take apart every book in my classroom, nor do I spend this much time with every discussion. The idea is to help readers slow down and notice more from the texts they read. I want to provide my students with extensive reading opportunities, but I also want the experiences students do have to be more beneficial. By revisiting the same book for a series of days, we are demonstrating to our students the power of rereading a book to make new and more extended interpretations. In our rush to introduce students to a wide array of literature, we inadvertently demonstrate to our students a read-it-and-move-on mentality. I want students to learn that revisiting a book can open up new discussions and that quality literature does not reveal itself in one reading. Quality literature must be savored and thought about and discussed.

FIG. L4.2
Books That Can Be Disrupted

Voices in the Park, by Anthony Browne

Where the Wild Things Are, by Maurice Sendak

Arrow to the Sun, by Gerald McDermott

The Watertower, by Gary Crew

Rome Antics, by David Macauley

Tuesday, by David Wiesner

Zoom, by Istvan Banyai

We Are All in the Dumps with Jack and Guy, by Maurice Sendak

Illustrated Quotes

The Challenge: Novice readers often have difficulty creating visual images in their heads as they are reading. Research has shown that readers who are able to create mental images are better at reading comprehension. Finding ways to help readers understand the types of images successful readers create in their heads when they read is challenging.

My Intentions: This series of lessons is designed to help readers create visual images in their heads about poems we are reading. By sketching the visual images we create from particular poems on paper, we can help readers understand how we visualize texts and how varied our interpretations can be.

Lesson Overview: While I read examples of descriptive poems, students will use pencil, charcoal, pastels, or markers to create sketches that represent the images they are creating in their heads. Beginning with the poem "Thunder Dragon," by Harry Behn, students will sketch a variety of images from different parts of the poem. Students will select particular quotes or stanzas from the poem and illustrate them for a wall display.

How It Might Go: Good morning, Readers! You might not know this, but readers who can deeply understand what they are reading can picture things in their heads while they are reading. It's like they create mind movies of the story as they read. Do any of you do this already when you are reading? [Discussion.] Well, today we are going to revisit one of our favorite poems. Remember "Thunder Dragon," by Harry Behn? Great! As I am reading the poem through the first time, I want you to close your eyes and see if anything comes to you as I read. [Read poem and discuss images in students' heads.] I am going to read this poem again and we will see if we can see any other mind pictures. When we are done reading the poem, I am going to provide you with art supplies and paper and we are going to see if we can make some sketches of what has been in our heads. This is not an art lesson. I don't care if you think you are a good drawer or not. We want to see if we can sketch what is in our minds and then talk about the different images we see.

Guided Practice: Occasionally, I have students respond in their literature response logs by sketching instead of writing. This supports students' multiple ways of understanding and allows them to express their interpretations in new ways.

Closing Comments: It is sometimes difficult for novice readers to describe what they see in their mind's eye when they are reading. Some readers may even tell us they don't see anything. Research has suggested that helping readers picture what they are reading helps them comprehend it. Being able to represent what one is thinking is an important skill. We have to find new ways to help readers represent their understandings.

Word Storms

The Challenge: Having a larger reading vocabulary helps one become a more successful reader. However, direct vocabulary instruction, done out of the context of reading, has proven to have limited effectiveness. In order to help novice readers develop an extensive vocabulary, we need to help them pay attention to language and inquire about words they don't know or understand.

My Intentions: By having students record particular words from a text being read aloud that are important to them and generating a list of words that they feel connect to the text, we can help students develop vocabulary knowledge within the context of an authentic reading event. In addition, word storms provide an opportunity to extend our discussions of the text. Whether vocabulary is caught or taught, unless readers attend to the words and language in a story, they will not expand their vocabularies.

Lesson Overview: Rather than brainstorm, students create a list of words, what I am calling a word storm, in order to make connections to the language and themes of a text. As I read a story aloud, students will make a list of words in their writer's notebooks that they feel are important to discuss. These words can come from the text or the students themselves but must relate to what they are thinking about the text. I ask each student to write down approximately ten words, then select three words from the list and write a brief paragraph describing why those words are important to the reader.

How It Might Go: Good morning, Readers! Today we are going to read a new picture book called *Zathura*, by Chris Van Allsburg (2002). This book takes up where *Jumanji* left off. While I am reading the book with you, I would like you to write down ten words about the book that seem important to you. These words can come directly from the story or they can come from your minds. Once we have the ten words written down, we are going to do something with them, but for now, let's read the story and see what words pop out for each of us. [Read story while students write down their words.] Now that we have our individual lists, let's share some of them with the class. I will write down some of the words that you have come up with. We may find that we have some of the same words on our lists. That's okay. [Create class list.] Now, I would like you each to go back to a writing spot and choose three of the words from your list or the class list and write a short paragraph discussing why those words are important. You will want to explain why those words connect to you and the story. Be ready to defend your choices to the class. Ready? Let's go!

Guided Practice: Sometimes, I will ask students to write a list of words in their literature response logs rather than write a regular entry. This reinforces the idea that I want students paying attention to language and vocabulary when they are reading.

Closing Comments: This lesson has direct connections to students' writing. As readers become writers, and begin to read like writers, they start to pay attention to the language and vocabulary of what they are reading. I have students keep these word storms in their writer's notebooks purposefully. In order for this to be a successful lesson, I need to model a word storm or two for the class. By thinking aloud as I read a book with my students, I can generate a Word Storm chart for them to see what I expect of them. This lesson works well with both fictional and expository texts.

Graffiti Boards

The Challenge: Because of the time novice readers spend in traditional reading instruction settings, they come to believe that it is their duty to tell the teacher what they think the teacher wants to hear about a text. Readers sometimes think the teacher has all the answers and that she knows what the main idea of every book is (and that there is *one* main idea hiding from them). Rather than tell us what they really think about a book, readers will often give us pat answers to get out of thinking for themselves. I often think that students believe as soon as someone in the class offers the correct idea, we can be finished with this discussion.

My Intentions: Using symbols, words, phrases, sketches, and other "graffiti," students will explore the variety of interpretations they construct during reading and share these interpretations with each other. I want students to come to realize that different readers come to understand texts differently, and that that is fine.

Lesson Overview: Using large sheets of butcher or chart paper, students will listen to a story or poem as I read it with them twice and write graffiti on the paper to represent their understandings of the text. Students will work in small groups to discuss, negotiate, and represent understandings. Then each group will share their ideas with the class.

How It Might Go: Good morning, Readers! Today we are going to try something new during our read-alouds. While I am reading one of our favorite stories to you today, I would like you to sit with a group of students and write some graffiti. Now, I know that when you hear the word *graffiti,* you think of spray paint on places where it's not supposed to go. However, the word *graffiti* comes from an Italian word meaning to scratch or write. The graffiti we are going to do today is going to be with markers, not spray paint, and it will be on paper, not on the wall, please. While I am reading our story aloud, I would like you to write down any words, phrases, symbols, sketches, or whatever comes to your mind. There is no correct answer to this project, just ideas we can explain to other readers. I know it's hard to listen to a story and do this, so I am going to read a book we have read a few times before so we can draw and listen. When we have finished, we are going to share our graffiti boards with the other groups. Okay?

Guided Practice: Sometimes, I will allow students to do graffiti in their literature response logs instead of a regular entry. Some educators have also called an independent graffiti board a sketch to stretch. As the groups are working on their graffiti boards, I circulate the room, offering ideas and taking notes on what they are putting on the chart paper.

Closing Comments: Like so many of these invested discussion practices, the goal is not to get good at graffiti boards, but to get good at discussing texts from new perspectives. One challenge with this lesson is that students often try to draw a picture from the book or copy other students in the small group. I want students to explore what is in their minds and represent those ideas on paper. This is not an art project and drawing skill should not deter readers from making interpretations.

Walking Journals

The Challenge: Students generally write in their individual literature response logs and rarely see or discuss how other students respond in their literature logs. Since we want our literature response logs to promote discussion and thinking about the texts we read, we have to find ways for these responses to become public, in the sense that other readers can read them and respond to them.

My Intentions: Using a journal that "walks" from reader to reader, students share their responses to texts and begin to develop an understanding of how other readers respond to shared texts.

Lesson Overview: After reading aloud a picture or chapter book, I write some responses and thoughts in a Walking Journal, a notebook that is specified as our shared response journal. When I am finished writing, I pass the journal to another student and invite him or her to read what I have written and respond to my thoughts and the book we have shared. The journal then walks from reader to reader throughout the class. From time to time I collect the journal and write another thought and read through what students have written.

How It Might Go: Good morning, Readers! Today we are starting an author study focusing on the work of Chris Van Allsburg, one of my favorite children's authors and illustrators. Each day we will be reading and discussing a book of his and creating our Impressions-Connections-Wonderings chart as we usually do (see Lesson 7.1). In addition to the charts we will be creating, we will be doing something new. I have here in my hands a special notebook I call our Walking Journal. Well, it doesn't exactly walk on its own, but readers walk it from one reader to another. When we have finished reading our first Chris Van Allsburg book, called *The Garden of Abdul Gasazi* (1979), I will write in the Walking Journal some of my impressions and responses to the book. When I am done writing, I will pass it along to one of you so you can read what I read. Whomever I pass it to, I expect that person to read what I have written, think about the book we read, and write a response in the Walking Journal. After that person is finished, he or she will pass it along to another person and so on. We will keep this journal on a special shelf that I made behind me. Anyone can pick up the journal and read it or write in it whenever he or she feels like it. I think it will be fun to read each other's ideas from time to time. I expect everyone to try writing in the journal once a month. I will read it each week to see how it is going and add some new ideas. Sound good?

Guided Practice: The Walking Journal provides an opportunity to scaffold students' response to selected books and demonstrate new ways of responding to texts. I have used the journal as an assessment device, meaning I learn about students as readers from it, but I would never grade it. If we don't remind students about the journal or keep modeling our responses in it, it will fade quickly. Once it is part of our classroom routine, we can assign one student to help keep it walking.

Closing Comments: I invite students to respond to the books being read and other students' ideas. They can make connections to other books and take the discussion wherever they like. I expect each student to read others' ideas as well as add one of his or her own.

The Literary Talk Show

The Challenge: Although novice readers are usually able to identify the main character in a story, they are frequently unable to describe the character in detail, understand his or her motives or perspective, or delve into his or her personality. When we read a piece of literature that contains an interesting character, we need to be able to enter the character's psyche to be able to relate to that character and predict how he or she might respond in certain situations.

My Intentions: Using role-playing techniques, students will get the chance to explore a character in depth and analyze how the character might respond to certain situations.

Lesson Overview: Using the format of a television talk show, like the *Late Show with David Letterman* or *The Tonight Show with Jay Leno,* students will assume the roles of literary characters and host and conduct an interview in front of the other students. The class will create questions for the host to ask and help the student-as-character decide how to respond.

How It Might Go: Good morning, Readers! Today we are going to try something new that might sound scary at first but should be a lot of fun once we get used to it. We are going to try some role playing, or acting as a character. We are going to choose some of our favorite characters from the picture and chapter books we have read and invite them to be guests on our *Literary Talk Show.* We are going to choose someone to be the host and someone to be a literary character from a story. Then, we are going to help those two people prepare for the interview and then we will do the show. Everyone will get a chance to be a host or a character this year if you would like to and we will rotate around in our jobs. There are three things we need to do and I will divide you into groups to get started. First, we need to decide which characters would be worth interviewing; second, we need to build a set for the show to take place; and third, we need to decide what kinds of questions the host might ask. Let's get started.

Guided Practice: Once students have seen how this works as a whole class, we can pair students up and have them interview one another as characters. The most important thing is not to force students into finding the *correct* way a character might respond, but to have them discuss how a character *might* respond.

Closing Comments: Providing opportunities to reflect on how this experience goes is critical. We need to evaluate whether the student-as-character responded appropriately to the host's questions. By discussing our ideas about how a character might respond, we are providing support for readers to understand and appreciate the characters in our favorite pieces of literature. During my years in the classroom, students that struggled in other literacy experiences shined as actors and in role-playing experiences. I have included drama techniques in many areas of the curriculum. I have also never been able to do things halfheartedly, so I usually end up building a set for the talk show and videotaping many of the episodes to watch later. Although the emphasis is on the literary characters, fun can be had along the way.

Readers' Theatre

The Challenge: Being able to engage with a piece of literature to the point where the reader is walking with the character through the events of the story is a prominent indicator the reader is not only comprehending the story but also deeply engaged with the story. Students can no longer simply read the words of the story. Readers must engage with the characters, envision the setting, imagine what the characters are feeling and thinking, and react emotionally as well as intelligently to the author's creation and enter into the story world.

My Intentions: I believe that if you can feel the emotions of the story, talk about it, act it out, explain it to someone that hasn't read it, create artistic representations about the story, and enjoy it, you've probably comprehended what you read. Using drama techniques and experiences, my goal in this series of lessons is to help novice readers enter into the story world, create interpretations of the story, and act these interpretations out with other readers.

Lesson Overview: This series of lessons begins with introductory drama techniques using picture books with relatively simple story lines to support children's interpretations of the story. As students get more comfortable with our acting experiences, I will begin to introduce more complex picture books and short stories. Adopting the role of characters in a piece of literature requires readers to first interpret the story, then decide how the characters would act in a skit or play.

How It Might Go: Good morning, Thespians! Have any of you ever heard the word *thespian* before? It is a Greek word that means actor. That's right, actors. We are going to use some simple acting experiences to try to make sense of some of the stories we have been reading. We will start with some simple picture books and give you the opportunity to act out the story. I have chosen some books that are easy ones to begin with. The characters in these stories talk a lot and it's easy to figure out how the story goes. Let's try a few.

Guided Practice: In small groups, I have students rehearse skits and interpretations from simple picture books. These are presented informally to the class and we can discuss how our interpretations may have differed.

Closing Comments: These skits are very informal. Trying to get students to act in front of other students can be a challenge. I have not written out a lot of direction in this lesson because of the ad-lib nature of these experiences. Beginning with some short jokes, skits, charades, and such, I try to get students used to acting, and I usually end the year with a complete production of a particular play.

FIG. L4.8
Books for Drama Activities

Yo! Yes?, by Chris Raschka

Where the Wild Things Are, by Maurice Sendak

There's a Nightmare in My Closet, by Mercer Mayer

Silly Sally, by Audrey Wood

STRAND 5

Developing Comprehension Practices

Helping children make sense of the texts they read should be the primary objective of reading instruction. In her seminal articles on reading comprehension, Dolores Durkin demonstrated that teachers traditionally *assess* comprehension, through questions and quizzes, more than they *teach* comprehension (see Durkin 1979). An important aspect of reading comprehension instruction is being able to make our own comprehension practices visible in order to help students understand how we, as competent readers, understand what we are reading. As fluent, capable readers, our reading comprehension practices are largely invisible to us. One of the primary challenges for us as teachers of reading is to learn to model our comprehension practices for our students.

The educational literature on reading comprehension that emerged in the 1980s and 1990s describes a series of reading strategies that proficient readers use. In addition, these research studies on reading comprehension instruction suggest that the comprehension strategies used by proficient readers can be effectively taught to novice readers. Many of the recommended reading strategies are included in this series of lessons.

Like many of the lessons described throughout this book, we need to be careful that readers don't become focused on the strategies themselves and forget that the purpose is to make sense of what they are reading. The comprehension practices described in this section are designed to help readers become more cognizant of the things they do when they are reading and thinking about a text. Although the practices described are cognitively focused, they are always conducted or implemented within a social context. The social context plays a prominent role in the construction and negotiation of meanings.

The comprehension lessons in this section include:

1. Visualizing What We Read
2. Asking Quality Questions
3. Monitoring Understanding
4. Summarizing Texts
5. Organizing Thoughts
6. Suspending Closure
7. Making Intertextual Connections
8. Drawing Inferences

Visualizing What We Read

The Challenge: Many novice readers tell us they aren't able to picture anything in their heads when they are reading (see Lesson 3.4 as well). Although this doesn't mean they aren't comprehending what they are reading, research suggests that readers who are able to visualize what they are reading—for example, characteristics of the setting, events in the story, or character traits—are better able to comprehend what they read. This comprehension practice is most effective when reading literature; we rarely visualize when reading an employment form or letter to the editor.

My Intentions: I want children to become deeply engaged with the texts they choose to read. In order to do so, readers must learn to enter the story world, walk alongside the characters to experience what the characters experience, and become emotionally connected to what the characters may be feeling. By describing to my students the images that are created in my head as I am reading a piece of literature or poetry, I can help novice readers learn to pay attention to the images they create and be better able to visualize the texts they read.

Lesson Overview: Reading descriptive poems about colors from the anthology titled *Hailstones and Halibut Bones*, by Mary O'Neill (1989), I will describe in this series of lessons the images that I create in my head as I read aloud to the students. I invite readers to close their eyes and share the images that come to them as they listen to these wonderful poems. Afterward, I ask the readers to sketch some of the images that came to their heads and share these with other students.

How It Might Go: Good morning, Readers! When you are reading a good book or poem, do you ever picture what the setting or the characters look like in your mind? [Discussion.] When I am reading, I try to make a picture or a movie in my mind. Sometimes, I even think about who would play the roles in the book if it were made into a movie. Do any of you ever do that? [Discussion.]

Today, I am going to read some very descriptive poems from the poetry book *Hailstones and Halibut Bones*, by Mary O'Neill. You may remember some of these poems from our unit in writing on poetry. As I am reading through several of these poems, I would like you to close your eyes and see what pictures you can create in your mind. After each poem is finished, we will share with each other some of the things that came to our minds. Don't worry if nothing comes to your mind; just relax and enjoy the poems I am reading. Something will trigger an image in one of these poems. For now, sit back, relax, close your eyes, and let your mind create some pictures as I read the poem about the color orange.

Guided Practice: I invite students to draw in response to their readings so we can discuss the images they are creating in their minds. These drawings are not an art project for students to try to match the technique of the illustrator if there is one. Rather, these sketches are designed to get students to expand their ideas, to explore new meanings as they are reading and sharing ideas with fellow readers.

Closing Comments: Some readers have told me that they are unable to create any images in their heads when they are reading. I am not sure if this is a sign of not being able to engage with a text or whether they didn't want to share what was in their heads in fear of being wrong. I believe that readers that can visualize what they are reading are better able to deeply engage with the texts they are reading. I think we need to cultivate readers' imagination and help them come to know the pleasures of seeing these mind movies when they are reading.

Asking Quality Questions

The Challenge: Novice readers often come to believe that when they read a text, they are supposed to understand everything and be ready and able to answer any questions the teacher may ask about the book. Traditionally, teachers were taught to assess comprehension by asking a series of literal and inferential questions after each selection was read. This traditional "teachers ask questions; students answer them" interaction still dominates the discussions being conducted in many classrooms in both elementary and secondary schools. This often leads to students trying to guess what is in the teacher's head. The teacher becomes the sole authority, positioned to check on whether readers are getting the main idea or not.

Readers need to learn to ask questions as they are reading, as much as try to understand what they are reading. We want readers to be able to ask quality questions that allow them to dig deeper into a piece of literature and analyze it from a variety of perspectives. As reading teachers, we cannot assume that readers know how to ask quality questions or understand what types of questions can be asked of a text. We must investigate the types of questions we ask and model for readers the types of questions that help us understand what we are reading.

My Intentions: By demonstrating for my students the kinds of questions I ask as I read a text, and explaining the differences between literal, inferential, and analytical questions, my hope is that readers will begin to ask these questions on their own as they read various texts.

Lesson Overview: This series of lessons is designed to introduce students to three different kinds of questions and show them where they should be looking to find the answers to these questions. First, literal questions ask the reader to look directly in the text for the answer. *Literal* means it is literally written in the text. These questions test memory more than comprehension and should be used sparingly, in my opinion. Inferential questions require the reader to infer some information from the world or their background experience and knowledge in order to answer them. In other words, the answers are not directly stated in the text and require the reader to synthesize information and think about relationships among ideas in the story. Analytical, or critical, questions require the reader to examine the text from different perspectives, including the author's intentions, the reader's background experiences, and sociocultural perspectives.

How It Might Go: Good morning, Readers! When I am reading a quality piece of literature, I often end up with more questions when I am done than answers. Is this okay, or should I have read it better? [Discussion.] I thought that experienced readers learned the answers when they finished reading, instead of generating more questions. I think that it is important for you to know that even people with Ph.D.'s that are old and smart like I am have questions when they read, and that it is okay to ask them and talk to other readers about what the answers might be. People have said for years that answers are easy; asking good questions is harder.

Most of the questions you may have seen on standardized tests or in textbooks usually have one correct answer and your job is to find it in the text, right? These are called literal recall questions and the answers are literally in the words of the text. For example, if I asked you what kind of suit Max was wearing in *Where the Wild Things Are*, you would say a wolf suit. It says so right in the text. There is only one right answer and you can find it by looking at the exact words in the story. Now, if I asked you why Max ran away from home to join the Wild Things, you could not find the answer right in the text. We would have to read the story and decide why he ran away. The answer is created in your minds by thinking about the text. These are called inferential questions because you have to infer. These are definitely harder questions. They make you think about the whole text and everything you know about the world.

A third kind of question, one that we have not even begun to ask very often, would be Why did Maurice Sendak write the book the way he did in 1960? We couldn't look at the book at all for that question. We would need to know something about the history of the book and what was happening when he wrote it. Or, I could ask you, Why was the main character, Max, a little boy, and how would the story have been different if it were a little girl? These are difficult questions, and like the inferential questions, they may not have one right answer. They may have several plausible or viable answers. That means we have to make a case for our answers. In other words, our answers have to make sense and relate to something in the book or in the world.

As we read some new books over the next few days, I am going to ask you some questions and I want you to think about whether they are literal, inferential, or analytical. What I want you to be able to do eventually is be able to create some of these questions yourself. It will take time, but you will get good at it.

Guided Practice: In pairs or small groups, I ask students to read a selection and generate examples of the three kinds of questions we have discussed. I tell them that asking the questions is more important now than answering them. We will discuss answers at a later time. We gather back together and discuss the kinds of questions we came up with.

Closing Comments: Different texts and different purposes make us ask different questions. I would not try to teach all of these questions in one lesson. The example I gave was just an introduction to the kinds of questions we can ask. It might work better with some groups to introduce just one type each day and create literal questions before trying the other kinds. I also go back to any Impressions-Connections-Wonderings charts I may have generated (see *The Reading Workshop* [Serafini 2001]) to analyze the kinds of questions we have asked of other texts we have read.

Monitoring Understanding

The Challenge: Successful readers are readers who make sense of what they read, are able to talk about what they have read, and continuously monitor their understandings to realize when things don't make sense and meaning has broken down. Unfortunately, novice readers often focus on decoding or oral fluency rather than making sense. The single most important practice a successful reader engages in is paying attention to what she is reading, realizing when things no longer make sense, and applying a reading strategy to get back to making sense of the text.

My Intentions: By describing what I do when I am reading and I get confused, and by thinking aloud as I read a text in front of my students, I can help readers understand how I monitor my comprehension. I want readers to be able to notice when meaning breaks down and what strategies they can use to make sense of their reading.

Lesson Overview: Using the metaphor of a mental VCR, I describe how I pay attention to the text I am reading and what I do when my reading no longer makes sense.

How It Might Go: Good morning, Readers! When I am reading a story, poem, or informational text, I am always paying attention to whether I am understanding what it is I am reading, and I hope you do, too. Sometimes, my mind starts wandering when I am reading and I get to the end of a page and realize I have no idea what I just read. Has this ever happened to you? [Discussion.] Well, don't worry—it happens to everyone, even experienced readers. The difference between a successful reader and an unsuccessful reader is, successful readers do something about it and unsuccessful readers just keep on reading.

One of my students from a few years ago told me that when he was reading, it was like a movie in his head and when he got confused, he just pressed the reverse button on the VCR, and when he got bored, he pressed the fast-forward button. Does that make sense to you? I thought it was a pretty good way to think about it.

Here is a good idea we can use to make sure that we are paying attention to what we are reading and that we are making sense of what we are reading. I call it Stop-Think-Share. What that means is, as we are reading along, at certain points we are going to stop reading, think about what we have read, and share some thoughts. When I am reading by myself, I can still use this strategy by writing some ideas in my notebook about what I have read up to that point. Here in class, we will stop and share with a reading partner.

I am going to demonstrate what I mean by Stop-Think-Share as I read the picture book *Home of the Brave*, by Allen Say (2002), to you today. At the end of each page, I am going to stop and think and then share some ideas with you. As we get going in the story, I may stop and ask you to share some thoughts, so you need to pay attention as well. If I get confused, if my brain is listening to my mouth and it doesn't make sense, I have to stop and do something. When that happens, we should talk about the possible things I can do to make sense of the text. Ready?

Guided Practice: I have students in pairs read a picture book with each other and stop at the end of every page, beginning with the title, cover, and other front matter, and share some thoughts. I wander around and monitor to see if they are using this practice to make sense of what they are reading together.

Closing Comments: In many ways, this is similar to think-aloud protocols and is quite useful as an assessment or research tool as well. I have tried what I called Retrospective Think-Alouds, where I tape-record students thinking aloud about a text and then play back for them what they said and ask them to comment on what they said as they were reading. This is an interesting new area of my research.

Summarizing Texts

The Challenge: Research suggests that readers who can summarize texts—in other words, are able to describe the gist of a story—do better on standardized measures of comprehension. Although higher test scores are not the only reason to demonstrate a particular reading strategy, I want readers to be successful on these measures of achievement. However, many readers think a summary is a condensed description of the plot of a story or the series of events in a story. The challenge for novice readers is to be able to describe in general terms what a story is about, to see the big picture of a story.

My Intentions: I want readers to be able to do well on standardized measures of comprehension, as well as be able to discuss texts from a variety of perspectives. Although I am reluctant to teach to the requirements of a test, I do believe that teachers should help students do well on standardized tests. One of the demands of a standardized test is the ability to summarize a story.

Lesson Overview: Using Library of Congress catalog descriptions and other authentic examples of story summaries, we will discuss what makes a story summary and work together to develop some examples. Beginning with three-sentence summaries, we will reduce the number of sentences down to one-sentence summaries and discuss what is eliminated.

How It Might Go: Good morning, Readers! This morning we are going to discuss summarizing a story and writing a summary statement. I am going to read one of our favorite stories, *Jumanji*, by Chris Van Allsburg (1981), and we are going to try writing a summary of the story. [Read story and discuss.] Okay, let's write down a few sentences that describe what the story is about. Anyone have an idea? [Students offer descriptive sentences.] Okay, let's look at the sentences and see if we can take the ideas and write a one-sentence summary. Then, we will look at the Library of Congress summary that can be found on the copyright page in many of the picture books we read. Then, let's look at what the book jacket says and read an advertisement I have for the book. Let's look at how they describe the story in one sentence.

Guided Practice: I ask students to work in small groups with selected picture books and write three-sentence, two-sentence, and one-sentence summaries. We discuss what we leave out each time and what stays in. I ask students to write a brief summary of what they read each night in their literature response logs. I use these homework assignments to assess who is able to write successful summaries and who needs more support. I also use some of the summaries in the response logs as examples of successful summaries and make transparencies to share with the class.

Closing Comments: I rarely ask students to do things with literature response activities that I can't find an example of in the world outside of school. Since I am able to find examples of summaries in the Library of Congress and in advertisements, I am able to demonstrate what they are like more effectively. There are many ways to write a successful summary. I believe that it is important to stress this fact to students; I don't want summary writing to become a contest to try to predict what the Library of Congress summary contains.

Organizing Thoughts

The Challenge: As the texts readers encounter become more complex, it becomes more difficult for novice readers to organize their thoughts across the reading of a book. The use of some prescribed graphic organizers imposes a structure prematurely on students' organization of thoughts. In other words, the organizer should fit the thoughts, not the other way around. Readers need to recognize the structure of the story in order to choose from a variety of organizers to represent their understandings.

My Intentions: I want students to be able to choose from a wide variety of graphic organizers to represent their thoughts about a story. The more versions of graphic organizers readers are familiar with, the better they will be able to choose one that fits their thoughts.

Lesson Overview: After reading several picture books aloud, the students will decide how to best represent their thoughts through graphic organizers. The graphic organizers I will introduce to students are the Venn diagram and other thinking maps.

How It Might Go: Good morning, Readers! When we are reading a book, sometimes it is hard to keep track of our thoughts. I was thinking that since we have been using some thinking maps in math and science, possibly these graphic organizers might help us keep track of our thoughts in our reading workshop. Let's start with the book *Tops and Bottoms*, by Janet Stevens (1995). I know we have read through this one before, but let's see if we can use any graphic organizers to represent our thoughts about the story. I am going to make three overlapping circles on a piece of chart paper. There are three major parts to this story, that is why I am making three circles. In each circle, we will describe one part of the story. In the intersection of the three circles we will put ideas that relate to the whole story. Okay?

Guided Practice: Students in small groups will work on selected picture books to represent their understandings of a story. Then we will share and discuss these as a whole group.

Closing Comments: This series of lessons is similar to the lesson on story structures (see Lesson 2.2). This time, we are using the graphic organizers to represent readers' understandings, not necessarily the structure of the story. Cause and effect, sequencing, and other traditional reading skills can be taught using different thinking maps. There are several new computer software programs that create webs and graphic organizers. These software programs offer new possibilities in representing students' thoughts and story structures.

Suspending Closure

The Challenge: Traditionally, readers have been taught to find the single main idea of a text when they are reading. This search for the one correct meaning forces readers to prematurely close down their interpretations and their construction of the possible meanings a text offers. Readers need to develop the ability to suspend closure, to think about the multiple possibilities a text offers, rather than reduce interpretations and discussion to finding the one "true" meaning of a text.

My Intentions: I want to help readers entertain ambiguity in their readings. When readers are able to deal with ambiguity and multiple meanings, they are better able to construct new meanings instead of reducing the possibilities to reach consensus. It is the unique interpretations that push our thinking about literature, not the commonly held ones.

Lesson Overview: Using a series of picture books that I have described as postmodern, readers will read and reread these books in order to construct multiple interpretations (see Figure L5.6). These books offer the reader ambiguity of meaning and contain elements that allow readers to widely interpret the text.

How It Might Go: Good morning, Readers! For the next few days we are going to read some weird picture books. I think they are great books, but some of you may think they are weird. They are certainly different. The books we are going to read have several different stories that overlap, or have different people telling their versions of the same event. These picture books are not like most of the books we have been reading, where there is one narrator or character telling a story that has a beginning, a middle, and an end. In fact, some of these books don't seem to have an end.

What is important in reading these books is not to get frustrated the first time you read them, but to be able to deal with ambiguity. *Ambiguity* means that there are things that aren't resolved, things that can be looked at in several ways in the story. We will have to read through these books several times in order to discover all of the possibilities they offer us. Don't decide too quickly what the books are about; instead, think of your first ideas as possibilities.

I know that many of you last year were asked in class to find the main idea of everything you read. Well, this year I am going to let you in on a secret: there is more than one idea in most of the books we read. In fact, there are several possibilities in each book that you could defend as main ideas. And you know, that's all right! Great books should have

Zoo, by Anthony Browne

Voices in the Park, by Anthony Browne

Black and White, by David Macauley

The Three Pigs, by David Wiesner

Bright and Early Thursday Evening, by Audrey Wood

Home of the Brave, by Allen Say

more than one idea in them. The challenge for us is producing or describing evidence that backs up what we think the ideas are. We have talked about this concept of defending your interpretations; now we will put it to work.

Guided Practice: After demonstrating how to read these postmodern picture books, I will provide numerous examples of these books and allow students to read, reread, and discuss them throughout the reading workshop. We will generate a definition for these unusual books and discuss ways to read them, ways to entertain ambiguity while we read. Throughout this unit of study, we will use the Walking Journal (see Lesson 4.6) and our response journals or book logs (see Lesson 7.1) to keep track of the many ideas that come to us and to explore the possibilities of these texts.

Closing Comments: If we want readers to construct multiple interpretations in transaction with a text, we need to read texts that contain ambiguous elements and multiple possibilities. The postmodern picture books I have selected are written using multiple narrators and perspectives. This technique does not privilege one version of the story over another. It is important for readers to be able to entertain ambiguity in order to revisit a selection several times and construct new and unique interpretations. The negotiation of meaning in a community of readers is the foundation of my reading workshop.

I believe that having the kind of literature I have described here as postmodern is vital to a reading workshop. I want students to be able to return to a text to construct new interpretations and negotiate the ones they constructed previously. It is through this suspension of closure and the providing of evidence for our interpretations that quality literature discussions ensue and comprehension is demonstrated.

Making Intertextual Connections

The Challenge: Research suggests that readers who are able to make connections among the different texts they are reading or have read—called intertextual connections—are better able to comprehend what they read. Since the book *Mosaic of Thought* (Keene and Zimmerman 1997) was published, many teachers have been talking about text-to-text, text-to-self, and text-to-world connections. For this series of lessons, I will be addressing the connections that Keene and Zimmerman described as text-to-text. When we read a novel or picture book, we use our understandings of every book we have previously read to make sense of the new book we are reading. Our understandings of the language of literature, literary conventions, and elements and structures of literature are generated by reading and sharing literature. By acknowledging these connections, we can help readers construct deeper interpretations of the texts they are reading.

My Intentions: By reading a series of picture books and a chapter book or two that are connected by a common theme, genre, or author, I will help readers understand what intertextual connections are and how they support our interpretations and understandings of the texts we read. If we want readers to make intertextual connections, then we need to read and discuss books that are connected.

Lesson Overview: Using the works of William Steig, we will conduct an author study that supports making connections across texts to help readers understand what constitutes an intertextual connection. Using an Emerging Categories chart, as described in my book *The Reading Workshop* (2001), I will demonstrate how these connections are made and what purpose they serve in comprehending new stories.

How It Might Go: Good morning, Readers! So far this year we have read several books by William Steig. We read *Sylvester and the Magic Pebble* (1988) and we read *Dominic* (1972) at the beginning of the year. I think it would be a good idea if we investigated more of his writing and his life to get to know this famous author through his writing. Each day for the next few weeks, I am going to read aloud some of his picture books and we will continue using our Impressions-Connections-Wonderings charts to keep track of our ideas. This time, instead of making only personal connections, I would like us to think about literary connections as we read his books. A literary connection, sometimes called an intertextual connection, is a connection between different texts. It can be a connection between a poem and a story, or a story and a story, or a movie and a story. They are all texts and they can be connected through similar ideas, characters, themes, settings, or other elements.

Let's begin a second chart that I will call an Author's chart. I will write down William Steig's name at the top, and as we start to get ideas about his writing and illustrations, we can include them on this chart. I have put out a notebook that contains as much information as I have collected about William Steig himself. I have some interviews and some information from newspapers and journals about him and his work. You are welcome to look through that notebook during workshop time if you like.

Today we are going to begin by reading *Dr. DeSoto* (1982), another one of William Steig's more famous books, and see if there are any connections between this book and the other ones we have read so far. Ready?

Guided Practice: I will invite students to read William Steig books on their own, in pairs, or in small groups over the next few weeks. Because of the extensive amount of work he has produced over the years, it is not possible to read every book, but I will try to have on hand as many of his books as I can find. I will also be reading aloud a chapter book, *Abel's Island* (1976), in addition to reading his picture books each day. Students will construct new response logs out of writing paper and construction paper, where we will keep our notes only about William Steig books. The author himself is the centralizing focus for this study, and students will be investigating his life and his work to understand how he writes and illustrates his books.

As the discussions around the books progresses, I begin to find emerging categories that come up again and again in our discussions. These categories become the headings across the top of a table, and the book titles become the headings down the side of the table (see Figure L5.7). This chart helps students make connections across texts but allows the categories to come from our discussions rather than be predetermined and imposed upon our discussions. For more details, read Chapter 4 of *The Reading Workshop*.

FIG. L 5.7
William Steig Emerging Categories Chart

May be copied for classroom use.
© 2004 by Frank Serafini, from
Lessons in Comprehension.
Portsmouth, NH: Heinemann.

Titles	Animals Used as Characters	Lessons Taught	Story Structure
Solomon the Rusty Nail			
Brave Irene			
Yellow and Pink			
Dr. DeSoto			
Sylvester and the Magic Pebble			
Abel's Island			

Closing Comments: If we choose to read favorite picture books each day that don't connect to each other, how can we expect readers to make connections across texts? By reading texts that are connected across genres, authors, themes, or topics, we are supporting readers to make intertextual connections. Reading a series of connected texts requires planning and the collection of resources before each day's reading commences. Intertextual connections help readers see the similarities among an author's work or different perspectives concerning a particular topic or theme.

Drawing Inferences

The Challenge: Novice readers often think all the answers to a standardized test question can be found by looking through the text itself. However, there are inferential questions that force the reader to read between the lines, to bring what he knows about the world to and draw inferences from the text in order to answer them. These are the most challenging questions for many readers, primarily because in school, readers are rarely asked what they think of a text and then provide evidence of their interpretations. Too many commercial assessments require literal recall and not inferential thinking. Readers come to rely on the text itself for all the answers and don't realize that the text speaks about the world as well. Readers need to be required to think beyond the boundaries of the text and be able to provide evidence about their interpretations.

My Intentions: As experienced readers, we naturally draw upon our understandings of the world as we interpret the texts we read. In this series of lessons, I want to demonstrate to readers how the ideas we construct come not just from the text but from our experiences and our knowledge as well.

Lesson Overview: Using the Impressions-Connections-Wonderings charts from a discussion of connected texts, I will point out how our ideas come from the text, the reader, and the world. Using three different symbols to represent the text (a book), the reader (a smiley face), and the world (a globe), I will help students analyze the kinds of ideas we offered in a particular unit of study. I will draw upon a unit of study we did previously, but any discussions chart would work.

How It Might Go: Good morning, Readers! Today, we are going to take a look at the Impressions-Connections-Wonderings chart that we created about William Steig (see Lesson 5.7) and we are going to analyze where the ideas came from. Some ideas come directly from the text; these we will mark with a little book. Other ideas come from our personal experiences; these we will mark with a little smiley face. The third kind of idea comes from what we know about the world; these we will mark with a world symbol. It is this third kind of idea, one that comes from the world, that we are going to pay attention to today. [Analyze and mark the chart.]

The comments or ideas on the chart that we marked with a world symbol are what we call inferences. We were using the ideas in the text and inferring about ideas outside the text. Let's take one of these ideas and see if we can show where this idea might have come from and if we can support the idea with information from the text and what we know about the world. For example, one of the comments we wrote down was that William Steig was concerned about friendship and how people treat each other. Does it say that directly in one of his stories? No, but we can show how we came to that idea. Let's take a few minutes and look through the chart and some of his books and see if we can find some evidence to back up the idea that William Steig cared about how people treated each other.

Guided Practice: Using a double-entry notebook, with an Ideas/Assertions column on one side and an Evidence column on the other, readers can make a point and then find evidence from the text, the world, or their experiences to back it up. It is the backing up of the idea that is the most crucial. I may do this activity with poetry: we would all read the same poem and provide evidence of our ideas before moving on to individual readings of particular poems.

Closing Comments: Having readers use information from the text and outside the text is crucial for helping them perform well on more sophisticated assessments. As long as our discussions privilege the text over our experiences as readers, assessments will continue to focus on literal recall and vice versa. In fact, I don't believe that literal recall should be used as evidence of comprehension. Literal recall is about memory, not about the reader's ability to make sense of a text. We need to help readers make connections among texts, their experiences, and the world if we expect them to comprehend what they read.

Investigating Informational Texts

About 90 percent of the texts used by classroom teachers during read-alouds are fictional or narrative in structure. Yet, approximately 60 percent of the books that intermediate- and middle-grade students check out from public and school libraries are expository or informational texts. In addition to this disparity, texts used in standardized tests are predominantly informational. As readers grow older, the reading materials they are required to read, and often those they choose to read, are informational materials. Because of this, it is important that classroom teachers begin to include reading instruction that focuses on informational texts to support the readers in their classrooms.

Informational texts provide unique challenges for both novice and experienced readers. Complex visual designs, multimedia graphics, expository writing, and a range of graphs, diagrams, maps, and visual aids make informational texts more difficult to read than narrative stories. Beyond textual structures, the prior knowledge needed to construct meaning with the demanding conceptual understandings discussed in informational texts requires new strategies for making meaning and new instructional approaches to support readers as they transact with these texts.

The comprehension lessons in this section include:

1. Determining Purposes for Reading
2. Previewing Informational Texts
3. Reading Visual Images and Components
4. Fiction Versus Nonfiction
5. Understanding Expository Text Structures
6. Evaluating Sources of Information
7. Inquiry Journals
8. Using a Table of Contents or Index

Determining Purposes for Reading

The Challenge: Novice readers approach an expository, or informational, text in the same manner, and often with the same reading strategies, that they approach a piece of fictional literature. As readers' purposes for reading vary, and the texts they choose to read change, so should the strategies and approaches they use for making meaning. Skimming over sections of a text and selecting which parts interest you may work well for reading the Sunday newspaper, but these same strategies will not work well for studying for an astronomy exam. Our purposes determine how we read. Helping novice readers articulate their purposes and what strategies may work best for those purposes will help them comprehend informational texts more effectively.

My Intentions: This series of lessons is designed to help readers understand the various purposes readers have for reading informational texts and how these purposes affect how readers approach a text.

Lesson Overview: Before reading an informational text, I will demonstrate to readers how to make a list of questions and areas of interest to guide our reading. We will discuss the various purposes we have for reading informational texts and which strategies may help us, depending on our purposes for reading. The list of ideas and questions we create will serve as a reading guide for that particular text.

How It Might Go: Good morning, Readers! When you choose a text to read, you usually have a specific reason or purpose for choosing that text, even if you don't say out loud what that reason is. We read for entertainment, to escape, to learn, to be able to do something, like cook a meal, or to find directions. Because we have different reasons, we approach texts differently. And, because we approach texts differently, we have different reading strategies for making sense of what we are reading.

Today, I am going to read from some different examples of informational texts. Each time I pick up a book, I am going to tell you why I am reading it. After I tell you why I am reading that book, you tell me what I should do. Okay? The first book is about Galileo and is called *Starry Messenger*, by Peter Sis (1996). I am reading it because I want to find out when he was born for a report I have been working on. What should I do? [Students offer suggestions like "Start at the beginning" or "Look in the table of contents."] What if I just wanted to read the book because I was interested in Galileo's life? Would I read it differently? [Discussion.] What if I wanted to read the book to make a time line of his life and other things that happened during that time period? Would I read it differently?

Let's look at another book, *Rome Antics*, by David Macauley (1997). This book is about a pigeon flying around Rome, Italy, trying to find his way home. If I was reading this book just to read a good story, I would probably start at the beginning and read it straight through. But, what if I was reading the book to find out about a particular building in Rome? What could I do then? Let's say I am doing a research project on Roman architecture; what questions might I ask before I begin reading? What things should I be looking for? [Make a list of topics and questions.]

Guided Practice: Although experienced readers do not always create a list of questions or topics to be investigated before they begin reading, if asked, they should be able to articulate their intentions. Because of this, I go around during our reading workshop and ask students why they are reading a particular text and how they approached that text, depending on their purpose. I want novice readers to approach texts differently, depending on their purposes for reading, and realize which strategies to draw upon to make sense of their texts, and I want readers to be able to discuss their purposes and strategies so that they will internalize this process.

Closing Comments: This lesson would continue with different books and different reasons for reading. Students would describe different approaches and we might make a chart for how to approach texts (see Figure L6.1). We read informational texts for a variety of reasons, from pure enjoyment to being able to answer questions on a test. The key to these lessons is being able to demonstrate how our purposes affect the reading strategies we use and the questions we ask of a text. I want readers to be able to articulate why they are reading a text so they will be able to understand what strategies may be most effective.

FIG. L6.1
Approaching a Text

❖ Skim through the pages first before reading.

❖ Look at the table of contents.

❖ Look in the index.

❖ Read the first page.

❖ Look through the illustrations.

❖ Look for chapter titles.

❖ Look at subheadings.

❖ Read captions under illustrations or photographs.

❖ Look for glossaries and other reading aids.

Previewing Informational Texts

The Challenge: After readers have determined their purposes for reading an informational text, they need to know how to approach the text, how to preview what is in the text to make their reading more efficient. Novice readers often open an informational text and simply begin reading on the first page and progress through the text as they would a piece of literature. Informational texts are not organized that way; in fact, many of them are not meant to be read from cover to cover. There are numerous design elements in informational texts, for example, the table of contents, index, glossary, chapter titles, subheadings, reading guides, and outlines, that help readers locate specific information. Readers need to learn how to effectively use these design elements and reading aids in order to become more effective readers of informational texts.

My Intentions: This series of lessons is designed to help readers deal with textbooks and informational texts in more effective manners. Many novice readers struggle when they begin reading expository texts because of the unfamiliar components included in them. By calling readers' attention to the various components of informational texts and demonstrating a process for previewing these texts, I hope to help readers become better able to comprehend informational texts and locate important information more efficiently.

Lesson Overview: Using selected informational texts and color transparencies made from particular elements in these texts, I will call to readers' attention various components of informational texts that they can use while previewing a text to get a sense of what is available in the book.

How It Might Go: Good morning, Readers! Remember when we talked about how to approach a piece of literature? We talked about reading the book jacket and other front matter before beginning the story. We talked about scanning through the illustrations to get a sense of the story. (See Lesson 3.3.) Well, we are going to do the same thing with some informational texts today. We are going to preview these texts in order to get a sense of what is contained in them so that when we go to read them or find specific things in them, we will be able to do that more effectively. Let me give you an example. I have here a book by Gail Gibbons called *The Moon Book* (1997). Based on the title, what do you think this book is about? That's right, the Moon. Would this be a good place to find information about dinosaurs? Obviously not! What about asteroids? Well, maybe. Asteroids and the Moon are closely related topics. But, it probably is a great place to find information about the Moon. We can begin by thinking about everything we already know about the Moon, or by making a list of questions we have about the Moon and then reading through the book to see what we can learn. However, what if I only needed to know about the phases of the Moon? Should I start at the beginning and just keep reading until I find out about that? Well, I guess I could, but I might be wasting a lot of my time. What else could I do? [Discussion.] Let's take a walk through this book and see what things in the text may give us clues to the kinds of information contained in the text and what we can expect from this book before we begin to read it.

Guided Practice: I will give the readers in each small group an informational text and allow them two minutes to preview the text and write down all the things they think will be contained in the text. At the end of the two minutes, I will ask each group to report back about where it looked to find clues about what was contained. We may make a chart of the group's suggestions and talk about any components the readers didn't use that may have helped them. Once we have discovered and investigated these components, I will make transparencies of each one (e.g., table of contents, index, etc.) and we'll discuss each in greater detail.

Closing Comments: Although the prior knowledge readers bring to a text is very important for making sense of what they're reading, being able to preview what is contained in a text helps readers approach it more effectively and efficiently. With the amounts of informational text reading increasing as students progress through each grade level, readers need to be able to preview a text to make their reading time most effective.

Reading Visual Images and Components

The Challenge: Informational texts contain illustrations, photography, charts, diagrams, and artwork that are designed to convey information. For many novice readers, these visual images may be confusing and present new challenges to understanding the information presented. Readers may attend to these visual images even more than the text at times but may have trouble understanding the information being conveyed or how to interpret the information. Readers need support in investigating these images and components and learning strategies for making sense of them.

My Intentions: This series of lessons is designed to call readers' attention to the various visual images and components contained in informational texts and demonstrate some strategies for making sense of these objects. I want readers to pay close attention to the illustrations, charts, and diagrams to get the most from their reading.

Lesson Overview: By making color transparencies of various images, charts, graphs, and diagrams, I will call readers' attention to the types of information available in these objects and provide them with some strategies for approaching them.

How It Might Go: Good morning, Readers! When you are looking through informational texts, I have noticed that many of you pay particular attention to the photographs and illustrations. Do you think about what the author or illustrator is trying to convey through the images, or do you just enjoy the pictures and move on? Come on, let's be honest! Well, I think we should talk about how to make sense of some of these things and start paying closer attention to what is contained in these components of informational texts.

Let's take a look at an Eyewitness series book about the desert (MacQuilty 1994). What kinds of components or types of images do we find in this text? Let's make a list (see Figure L6.3). Each day, during our unit of study on informational texts, we are going to look at one of these text components and talk about how to read it and what kinds of information we can learn from it.

FIG. L6.3
Visual Images Contained in Informational Texts

May be copied for classroom use.
© 2004 by Frank Serafini, from
Lessons in Comprehension.
Portsmouth, NH: Heinemann.

- photographs
- charts
- graphs
- captions
- sketches
- bulleted lists
- legends and map guides
- cross-section diagrams
- introductions or author's notes
- diagrams
- maps

- headings
- labels
- information or fact boxes
- sidebars
- flowcharts
- time lines
- tables
- pronunciation guides
- reading guides
- bold or italicized print

Guided Practice: After I have introduced these components to the whole class, I will have students work in small groups with different components and answer the following questions:

1. What is the subject of the component?
2. Why do you think the publisher put it in there?
3. What can you learn about the subject in this component?
4. How is the information presented?
5. What is challenging about reading this component?
6. What strategies would you suggest for other readers?

We then gather back together and each group can present its component and how the readers approached it and answered the questions. We create a chart about how to read each component and refer to this chart throughout our study. This chart may even become an informational reading strategies bookmark, similar to the one we created for our navigation strategies (see Lesson 3.1).

Closing Comments: Many novice readers are confused by these components. Their confusion is often created by inexperience with these images rather than a lack of background knowledge. I want readers to approach these components and ask themselves what is it that they are trying to tell the readers. I use color transparencies of different images and components to talk about what is contained in the various components and how to make sense of them. These are important discussions that help readers learn how to approach informational texts.

Fiction Versus Nonfiction

The Challenge: The boundaries that divide fictional literature from nonfiction materials are blurry. Books that are described as nonfiction often contain fictional elements, for example, the Magic School Bus series, and factual information can be found in fictional literature, especially historical fiction. Authors of historical fiction spend a great deal of effort researching their subject matter to present a realistic portrayal of the times they use for their narratives.

Relying on the terms *fiction* and *nonfiction* may focus on the wrong distinctions between the two types of writing. Fiction versus nonfiction is based on a relationship between reality, the way things really are, and what we know about that reality. In other words, do the facts in the book relate to the way things really are in the world? However, the way things really are is always changing and what was once an accurate portrayal of particular events may become quickly outdated or completely erroneous.

The terms *narrative* and *expository* or *informational texts* may be better descriptors of the distinctions I want readers to make between these two types of texts. These terms are based on the way the text is organized, how it is written, and what the text is intended for, not the truth value of the information contained therein. Narrative structures—stories containing characters, plots, and settings—are most common to young readers. Narratives tell a story and generally take place across time. Expository texts are not always sequentially ordered and are designed to convey information using different textual structures. The intentions of these texts are inherently different, so the structures they use are different.

My Intentions: Throughout these lessons, I intend to call to readers' attention the various structures and intentions of expository, or informational, texts. I want readers to be exposed to expository structures and to provide an opportunity to discuss how they differ from the more common narrative structures children read and listen to. It is important that we help readers develop reading strategies that are effective for making sense of these informational text structures.

Lesson Overview: In this series of lessons, I will use outdated examples of nonfiction texts to help readers question the truth contained in nonfiction. I want to blur the distinction between fiction and nonfiction and introduce the concepts of narrative and expository structures as a better way to distinguish between the two types of texts. In addition, I want students to be able to discuss the differences between narrative structures and expository structures in order to understand the various reading strategies that are effective for making sense of different texts and structures.

How It Might Go: Good morning, Readers! What is the difference between fiction and nonfiction? [Students generally offer the idea that nonfiction is true and fiction is imaginary.] Well, if that is accurate, then I am somewhat confused! You told me that the Magic School Bus books were nonfiction because they contained facts, but there is also a flying school bus in many of those stories. I didn't know that school buses could fly!

I have a book here called *You Will Go to the Moon*, by Mae Freeman (1971). In this book it says that someday man may be able to go to the Moon. What do you think about that? Haven't we been to the Moon? Depending on when a book is written, things that are true may change. Before Galileo did his experiments, it was true that the Sun went around Earth. Of course, now we know that Earth goes around the Sun.

When we are reading fiction, sometimes don't we learn about the way things are or were? When we read *Nightjohn*, by Gary Paulsen (1993), didn't we say that we learned a lot about what it would have been like if we were slaves? Well, wasn't that a fictional book?

I have a suggestion for what might help us clear up the issue. *Nightjohn* was a historical narrative, meaning it had a plot, characters, and a setting. Most nonfiction books, not counting the Magic School Bus series, don't have characters. They are written to convey information, not to tell a story. Narratives tell a story; informational, or expository, texts are written to expose us to information. Maybe we should think about organizing our library into narratives and informational texts, rather than using *fiction* and *nonfiction* as labels.

When we read narrative stories, we follow along with the characters and experience the things that they experience. There is a setting and a plot, and we pay attention to what is happening in the story to anticipate what might happen next. If we try this with an informational text, we will probably get confused. In fact, there are some informational texts that aren't meant to be read from front to back, like atlases, reference books, and encyclopedias. We have to learn how to approach these texts differently and what they are designed to do for us as readers.

Guided Practice: I want readers to notice that narrative and expository texts contain different elements, and that both of these may be able to convey information in different ways. We generate a chart explaining the differences between the two kinds of texts (see Figure L6.4). Because of this, I often require that expository texts be read for homework as well as novels. I want students to spend time reading both and come to understand how authors create each of these texts. We practice locating information and talking about how informational texts differ from stories.

FIG. L6.4
Narrative and Expository Text Structures

May be copied for classroom use.
© 2004 by Frank Serafini, from
Lessons in Comprehension.
Portsmouth, NH: Heinemann.

Narrative Structures	Expository Structures
Have characters, setting, and a plot	Usually have no characters and no plot
Tell a story	Explain/present information
Make you turn the page by creating suspense	Make you turn the page because you are interested in the topic
Have paragraphs and chapters	Have headings and sections
Use story language	Use special vocabulary
Are like telling a story	Are like a news report
Use pictures to tell parts of the story	Use diagrams to explain things

Closing Comments: Things and knowledge change. In future lessons, we will have to address how to evaluate the sources of information presented (see Lesson 6.6). For now, talking about the differences between narratives and expository texts makes more sense than arguing about the truth value of the information provided. This change in focus, talking about narratives and expository structures, helps readers attend to the differences in the texts they read and signals to them that these texts need to be read differently.

Understanding Expository Text Structures

The Challenge: As described in Lesson 6.4, expository structures are different from narrative structures and pose new challenges for novice readers. Most young readers are predominantly exposed to narrative structures and are challenged by the conceptual requirements, unfamiliar vocabulary, and unique structures of expository texts. Aside from the components that are included in informational texts, for example, diagrams, sidebars, and captions, expository texts are written differently. There are numerous ways that expository texts are organized and written. Helping readers attend to these structures and understand how these texts are organized will help them become more successful readers of informational texts.

My Intentions: In this series of lessons, I will demonstrate the various ways that the written text in expository, or informational, texts is organized using selected portions of contemporary informational texts. By analyzing the various written structures of these texts, readers will learn how to recognize, approach, and use informational texts more effectively.

Lesson Overview: These lessons will focus on the various structures of expository writing, for example, question-answer, cause-effect, problem-solution, refutational texts, descriptive accounts, and texts that are chronologically sequenced. I will use examples taken from informational texts that students are acquainted with and have been available in our classroom library. We will analyze how these texts are constructed and what clues about the written structures are available to help readers make sense of these texts. We will discuss how to approach these texts and which reading strategies would be most effective for locating and understanding the information presented.

How It Might Go: Good morning, Readers! You probably have noticed during this unit on informational texts that these texts are written differently than the stories we have been reading in our other units, especially fairy tales and poetry. Most narrative stories have a beginning, a middle, and an end, but informational texts can be organized differently. Sometimes there are questions written in bold letters and answers provided below the questions. Sometimes, the information is presented along a time line, in chronological order. And other times, there are several causes and an effect presented. Today, we are going to look at the different ways informational texts are written and what reading strategies may be most effective for understanding them.

Guided Practice: I often have readers work in small groups to investigate different text structures that focus on the same topic or subject. For example, I may have small groups all read different texts about the Grand Canyon. Brochures, picture books, maps, informational texts, magazines, and travel guides all present information about the Grand Canyon in different ways. We would talk about what we learned from the different texts and then we would talk about how we found that information in the texts. The primary focus of these particular lessons is the strategies we use to makes sense of these texts, concentrating on how the texts are organized, not necessarily on the information presented.

Closing Comments: To assume that readers know how to approach these different textual structures would be a mistake. Exposure to informational texts is important but insufficient for providing readers with effective strategies for approaching these texts. Teachers need to understand and recognize how information is presented in the expository texts available for their students and learn ways to call students' attention to these textual structures. Each textual structure requires different reading or note-taking strategies. Only by direct demonstrations can we help readers acquire the strategies needed for making sense of informational texts.

FIG. L6.5
*Informational Text
Structures*

May be copied for classroom use.
© 2004 by Frank Serafini, from
Lessons in Comprehension.
Portsmouth, NH: Heinemann.

❖ *Descriptive*—Describes specific details about a concept or object using adjectives and visual information.

❖ *Refutational*—A myth or misinformation is presented and then refuted in order to help readers discover their misunderstandings.

❖ *Cause and Effect*—An effect is presented along with possible causes. Science and history texts are frequently written this way. Gives reasons or explanations for particular events or phenomena.

❖ *Compare and Contrast*—Two related events or objects are presented. The characteristics of the two objects or events are outlined and readers are invited to note the similarities and differences.

❖ *Problem-Solution*—A problem and one or a series of solutions is offered.

❖ *Question and Answer*—A question is posed and an answer is provided.

❖ *Chronologically Sequenced*—Events are presented in the order they occurred across time.

Evaluating Sources of Information

The Challenge: Texts and authors often disagree on facts and information. Not all information presented in informational texts is accurate or timely. Therefore, it should not be given the same value by the reader. However, how are readers to learn to evaluate the reliability or accuracy of the information they are presented? Helping readers evaluate the sources of information presented is challenging. Many readers believe that if it is written in a book, it must be true. Most textbooks provide no sources, only facts, and are generally written in a way so as not to allow readers to question what they say.

My Intentions: I want readers to question everything they read. I want them to evaluate every piece of information and hold it tentatively, pending further investigation. In order to do so, I have to present conflicting information to get students to wonder what is going on. As Paulo Freire stated (Freire and Macedo 1987), readers need to learn to read the world as well as the word. Informational texts provide a good place to get started.

Lesson Overview: In this series of lessons, I present readers with conflicting information about a particular topic that is of interest to students. Using newspaper accounts, editorials, magazines, and textbooks, I present students with different accounts so they have to decide which information is more trustworthy. We discuss the various criteria we can use to make our evaluations.

How It Might Go: Good morning, Readers! Let me read to you two different explanations, from two different sources. In this textbook, it says that in 1492, Columbus discovered America. He landed in the West Indies and conquered the islands in the name of Queen Isabella and King Ferdinand of Spain. In the book *Encounter*, by Jane Yolen (1992), it says that Columbus landed on the same islands and murdered the people that were there and stole their treasures. Which version of history is true? Can they both be accurate? How can we tell which one to believe?

This is one of the biggest challenges we will have as readers of history and other informational texts. How do we evaluate the information presented to us? I want to talk to you today about some criteria I use when I am trying to evaluate information and discuss these with you to see if they make sense and whether we should use them when we are reading informational texts and other materials.

When I am reading a text, particularly an informational text, I think about these things:

1. Who wrote it? What right does this person have to talk about this subject? How reliable is this person? What is his or her reputation?

2. Where is the information coming from? Primary or secondary sources? How old is the information?

3. How many perspectives are offered? One point of view or many?

4. Where is this information located? In what magazine, book, reference material? How much authority does this location have?

5. What is the author trying to make me believe?

6. What do I know about this topic already?

Let's take another look at the two explanations of what happened with Columbus and apply these criteria to see if that helps us understand this information.

Guided Practice: The six criteria and questions in the previous list become a chart in our room that we use to evaluate the texts we are reading. In small groups, I often have readers read a variety of perspectives on the same topic and then we debate the merits of each perspective. I am not trying to get readers to draw specific conclusions; rather, I want them to learn to question what they read and apply the criteria on our chart.

Closing Comments: One of the best ways to do this activity is to get information about a subject from newspapers from a different country than the Unites States. How events are portrayed in foreign newspapers can differ quite dramatically from how U.S. papers portray events. Getting readers to question information takes time and requires an extensive understanding of the information being discussed. It's hard to critique things we know very little about. Because of this, I believe that we must begin these lessons with topics that are familiar and important to our students.

Inquiry Journals

The Challenge: Keeping track of the vast amount of information collected on some of the research and inquiry projects students generate can lead to confusion and poor organization in their writing. Helping readers organize the information they collect, ask questions that lead to further inquiry and understanding, paraphrase the information collected, and evaluate the information they collect will help them write higher-quality reports and understand their world better.

My Intentions: By introducing students to a version of an inquiry journal that I have used for my research, I will demonstrate for readers one way to organize their information and keep track of their inquiry projects.

Lesson Overview: In this series of lessons, I demonstrate the use of a particular type of journal writing, which I describe as an inquiry journal. This journal includes the following headings: Facts, Source of Information, Connections, Reliability Rating, Questions, and Comments.

How It Might Go: Good morning, Inquirers! You probably have noticed when I am reading, I often keep my writer's notebook next to me so I can take notes on things that interest me. Today, I am going to share with you how I organize the journal that I use when I am doing research. I call this my inquiry journal and use it to collect and evaluate information as I come across it.

In my inquiry journal, I have several categories or headings that I think about when I am doing my research or observations (see Figure L6.7). First, I have a column for the facts as they are written down in the book. I usually copy them exactly as they are written, knowing I will change the wording later. In the next column, I make a note about where this information came from, or the source of the information. I use the third column to connect this information to other facts I have already gathered. This column helps me think about what I am learning along the way. The next column is where I give the information a rating. Like the movie rating we see on television, I give the information one to three stars, depending on how good I think the information is. The last column is for any questions that come to me as I am doing my research. This is an important column because it gives me direction for where I am headed. Let's read through an informational text and see how this journal works.

FIG. L6.7
Inquiry Journal Example

May be copied for classroom use.
© 2004 by Frank Serafini, from
Lessons in Comprehension.
Portsmouth, NH: Heinemann.

Facts	Source of Information	Connections	Rating (***)	Questions
Columbus discovered America in 1492.	history textbook	This goes against what many other sources have told me. This is what we traditionally think about Columbus.	One star * Only one perspective offered.	Who wants us to think Columbus discovered America? Why do we celebrate Columbus Day? Was Columbus a bad guy?

Guided Practice: I have students try using the inquiry journal for their independent research projects. We may revise these journals to meet our needs, but students are required to address the categories I specified when they are researching topics.

Closing Comments: Theoretically, I believe that information is constructed, not simply found. However, for ease of explanation, we begin by discussing where we find it and then how we evaluate it (see Lesson 6.6). Students choose which facts to attend to and evaluate the trustworthiness of each. In this way, they are constructing understanding, not discovering it prepackaged. I demonstrate the use of this journal with some examples of informational texts that students are using for their research.

Using a Table of Contents or Index

The Challenge: There are components of informational texts that are included to help readers find information and illustrations. Two of these are the table of contents and the index. Unfortunately, novice readers usually skip over these reading helpers to get at the text. Informational texts are generally not meant to be read from cover to cover. Rather, they are designed for readers to pick and choose what is important to read. Helping readers use the tools provided will make their reading of informational texts more efficient and successful.

My Intentions: By providing several examples of tables of contents and indexes from various informational texts, I will expose novice readers to a variety of reading guides. I want to demonstrate how I use these guides when I approach informational texts and how readers can use them to make their reading time more effective.

Lesson Overview: I will make overhead copies of several different tables of contents and indexes from informational texts. I will share each one with my students and discuss what information can be found there. We will use these discussions to create a chart for using the guides provided in information texts.

How It Might Go: Good morning, Readers! When you open an informational text, do you usually skip right to the first page of text or the illustrations? Yes, you do, I have watched you do it. There are a couple of things included in an informational text that may help you find the information you are looking for. Do you know what any of these may be called? That's right, the table of contents and the index. I have made some overhead copies of some tables of contents and indexes for us to look at today. What I would like you to do is look at the table of contents I put up on the overhead and tell me what you notice. Let's look at how it is organized and what is included. Then we will do the same for some indexes.

Guided Practice: I will ask students in pairs or small groups to look at the table of contents and index in a book they are reading and then report back to the class what they have found. We will use a list of questions I have created to help guide their exploration of these two reading guides (see Figure L6.8).

FIG. L6.8
*Questions for Exploring
Tables of Contents
and Indexes*

May be copied for classroom use.
© 2004 by Frank Serafini, from
Lessons in Comprehension.
Portsmouth, NH: Heinemann.

1. How are the TOC and the index organized?

2. What do you think may be included in some of the chapters based on their titles?

3. What types of labels are used to locate information?

4. Which reading aid has more specific information? Why?

5. How are they different?

Closing Comments: You can certainly read an informational text without using either the table of contents or the index, but when you are looking for something specific, they are invaluable resources. These two resources are not hard to figure out, but there are some clues readers need to understand. For example, in an index, when a word or page number is in italics, it usually means there is an illustration on that page. Also, indexes are ordered alphabetically and tables of contents are in page order.

Extending Response to Literature

As teachers of reading, we often focus on what readers do *after* they finish reading, rather than on what occurs during the reading event. Workbooks and commercial novel units contain numerous activities designed to extend readers' experiences with a particular text by having them create mobiles, book reports, or inauthentic writing assignments. Some of these activities seem to have little or no connection to the actual literature being read or the students doing the reading. Traditional reading programs have required our students to write three-paragraph book reports, turn cardboard boxes into dioramas, and answer literal recall questions after reading each chapter to prove to teachers they have comprehended what has been read. These activities have such a superficial connection to the texts being read that I often wonder where the designers of these activities got their ideas. However, in the world outside of schools, when we finish reading a story or book, we naturally do one of the following: share the book with a friend, read another book by the same author or about the same topic, write some ideas in a notebook, reread the same book again, or simply enjoy the story and put it away.

In this section, I want to share with you some of the response strategies that I feel help individual readers deepen their understandings of a text. These response activities are designed to help readers generate and extend meanings after they read and negotiate these meanings with other readers. I believe that each of these may provide robust, rather than superficial, connections to the text being read and is somehow connected to the things that readers naturally do with texts in the world outside of school.

The comprehension lessons in this section will include:

1. Literature Response Logs
2. Letters to Authors and Illustrators
3. Multigenre Writing Projects
4. Books-to-Music Connections
5. Responding to Our Responses
6. Evaluating Responses
7. Reader's Chair
8. Reader Profile

Literature Response Logs

The Challenge: Asking students to write about what they have read has been a tradition in school for the past few centuries. Traditionally, students have generated book reports for each book read so teachers could assess their comprehension and make sure they read the required materials. I have used literature response logs in my classrooms every year that I have been a teacher. There are instances when I feel that my students have interpreted this assignment as a traditional book report and have simply written in their logs to appease me or follow directions. The challenge with literature response logs is helping students understand that this is a space for them to reflect and think about what they have read and to share their ideas with me.

Over the years, I have predominantly used literature response logs as a homework assignment. I model their use in the classroom, but I require students to read for thirty to forty-five minutes each night and write in their response logs. Each student then shares his or her log in the morning with another student and I collect them once a week so I can respond to readers' ideas.

I want readers to use their response logs to extend their understandings, to probe new ideas, and to share their thoughts with their lit log partners and with me. In order for the literature response logs to be successful, readers need to know that this is a place for them to think, ask questions, and share their ideas, not guess what is in the teacher's head.

My Intentions: I want students to begin to use their literature response logs as a place to think, to wonder about what they are reading, and to share their thoughts with other readers in our community. In order to have them do so, I have to demonstrate how these logs work, what the required format is, when we write in them, and what a quality entry may look like. This takes time and constant modeling and monitoring. The closer we can align the format of the literature response log with the types of response strategies we use in the classroom, the more successful readers will be.

Lesson Overview: This series of lessons will introduce students to literature response logs, demonstrate how they are used, and offer them a framework for responding to their readings. These response logs must become a part of our classroom and be used for our discussions; otherwise, they will become glorified book reports. One way to avoid this is to provide response to students' thinking on a daily basis from other readers and a weekly basis from the teacher.

How It Might Go: Good morning, Readers! I have been asking you to take home a book to read each night for about thirty minutes. So far, it seems like everybody has been able to do that for the first two weeks of school. We have organized the library so you can check out a book and when you line up to go home, you are able to tell me what you are reading each night. This is great.

Now we are going to add something to our homework. In addition to our math packets and our time for reading in our lives, I want you to start writing in what I have called a lit log. These lit logs look a lot like the Impressions-Connections-Wonderings charts we have been doing during our read-aloud discussions already. I am going to read another chapter from our read-aloud book today, and then we are going to fill in a whole-class lit log so you can see how this works. After a few days of trying this together, we are going to make our own lit logs and begin taking them home to write in after we read each night.

Every morning when you come in to school, you are going to share your lit log entries with a lit log partner. You are going to choose someone to share with. If you and your partner do a good job, you can work together until Winter Break. If you start fooling around, or you don't write in your logs, either I will assign you a new partner or you will share your log with me every day. Our lit logs are very important. I use these logs to help me understand what you are thinking about when you read. We are going to talk about them for a few weeks, and we are going to do one together in class for awhile. I will even make overhead copies of some entries from your lit logs that I think are well done and we will talk about them as a class. Any questions before we begin? Okay, I want you to pay close attention to our read-aloud today so that you can offer some ideas to put into our class lit log example. Ready?

Guided Practice: Each night students will take these logs home and write about what they are thinking as they read. Each morning we will talk about how they went and offer suggestions for doing them better. I provide a format for us to use as we begin (see Figure L7.1), but this may change or remain the same over the course of the year. It depends on how well it supports our thinking. Response to students' efforts in their logs is important if we are going to use them to extend their thinking. If we don't read them and write back to students, the logs will, in fact, become glorified book reports. Students need to learn that we honestly care about what they think and we are providing a place for them to share their ideas.

Closing Comments: Modeling, demonstrations, discussions, and attention to the logs as we get started are crucial if these are going to be successful with our students. The entries that my students write in September are not as good as the ones they write in January. We have to be patient and realize that as our whole-group discussions get better, our lit logs will get better. If students can't make connections or offer impressions as a whole group, what

FIG. L7.1
Literature Response Log Format

May be copied for classroom use.
© 2004 by Frank Serafini, from
Lessons in Comprehension.
Portsmouth, NH: Heinemann.

Name: _____   Date: _____

Title/Author of Book: _____

How Long I Read For:

Impressions:

Personal Connections:

Literary Connections:

Wonderings (Questions):

Any Other Ideas:

makes us think they will be able to do it on their own or in literature study groups? The demonstrations, reflections, and discussions we have as a whole group provide the foundation for the lit logs.

It is important that students understand what is expected of them for homework and that they feel successful doing it. Parents should be informed about your expectations for homework, and a letter detailing those expectations can alleviate a lot of tension at home. Every student is expected to have a chapter or picture book to read each night for homework. The books may come from the classroom library, school library, or public library. The purpose of the literature response log is *response*; therefore, I allow approximated spellings in these logs because the point is reflective thinking, not published writing. It is important to convey this to parents as well to avoid confusion and to avoid losing the purpose of these response logs.

Letters to Authors and Illustrators

The Challenge: Young readers sometimes think books simply appear on the shelves of our libraries. Unless they are familiar with the work of particular authors, they probably don't understand the processes involved in creating books. I believe it is important to acknowledge authors and illustrators of children's literature and find ways to investigate their histories and make them come to life in our classrooms. Questioning what an author was thinking about when he was writing a book helps readers understand the author's perspectives and worldviews. Once readers realize that people write books, they can begin to question what is included in them. By allowing novice readers to write letters to the authors and illustrators of their favorite books, we are acknowledging the process of creating children's literature, and we are also lending credence to our students' opinions and ideas.

My Intentions: I want readers to know that what is written in books is not dogma, that it can be questioned and that authors' perspectives can be disagreed with. In order for readers to be able to question authors, they must realize that people write the books they read.

Lesson Overview: I ask students to choose an author that has written a book we have read recently and write a letter to him or her. Each letter should include some specific questions and ideas about the author's work. As an author myself, I appreciate specific comments and questions about my work. When readers write to me, it allows me to further explain my ideas or intentions.

How It Might Go: Good morning, Readers! We have talked a little about some of the authors and illustrators of the books we have been reading. I have shared with you some of the brochures, webpages, interviews, and newspaper clippings I have collected on particular authors. Now it is time for you to do some investigating on your own. I want you to choose an author or illustrator whose work has influenced you as a writer or a reader and write a letter to him or her. We are not going to simply write letters asking for pictures or autographs. We are going to write intelligent letters asking authors or illustrators particular questions about their work in order to understand why they do what they do. In order to write a good letter, you will need to explore the person's work in depth and think about some good questions to ask. We will get together next week and share some of our questions to see what we should ask. For now, let's begin by deciding which author or illustrator you would like to write to.

Guided Practice: Students can write letters to their favorite authors and illustrators on their own any time they like. Visiting author and illustrator webpages can also be a good resource for investigating their work.

Closing Comments: If we want readers to eventually question the opinions and perspectives of authors, they need to first understand that books are created by authors. People write literature; it does not simply appear in our libraries. Students can learn a great deal about their favorite authors by visiting their webpages and writing letters to them. This is a surefire way to help students pay attention to who is writing the books they are reading.

Most authors have extensive websites for readers to investigate their work and lives. As readers come to learn about their favorite authors, they may develop questions to ask and ideas to explore with them. Most authors accept letters through their publishers or directly from interested readers. My students have received promotional packets including photos and illustrated materials. To their credit, I have not had a student write to an author and not hear back from them. My students get very excited to receive information from their favorite authors, and we celebrate when things arrive.

Multigenre Writing Projects

The Challenge: Readers need to learn that different genres fulfill different expectations for readers. Each particular genre uses literary elements in unique ways and has a different structure and format. One way to help readers understand these concepts is to read across many genres. Another way to help readers understand the differences is by inviting them to respond to a piece of literature by transforming the idea from one genre into another genre. For example, after reading the book *Where the Wild Things Are* (Sendak 1963), I invited my students to explore their responses and interpretations of the text by creating related pieces of writing. Students wrote missing-person posters asking for Max's safe return, eulogies for the Wild Things, travel brochures for exploring the imaginary island, a Wild Things rap, birthday party invitations for Max's birthday, and advertisements for purchasing a scepter and a crown. All of these responses were closely related to the original story. As students transposed the story into new pieces of art and writing, they represented their interpretations of the original story in new ways and expanded their understandings of the text.

My Intentions: By inviting readers to respond to a particular story by writing new texts in a variety of genres, I am helping them understand how different genres work and explore their responses to a particular story. I want readers to take the ideas, themes, and language of the original story and create a parallel piece of writing that expands their understandings of the original story.

Lesson Overview: After reading and discussing *Where the Wild Things Are* for several days (see Serafini 2001 for a more detailed explanation and examples of different responses), I invite students to take the characters, plot, setting, or themes from the story and create a new, parallel piece of writing in a different genre. I ask students to explain the connections made to the original story.

How It Might Go: Good morning, Readers! We have been discussing the book *Where the Wild Things Are* for several days now. I think we have had some great discussions and have come to new understandings of this imaginative story. Another way to respond to this story is to take the ideas, characters, or setting and write about it in a different genre. Let me give you a couple of examples. First, we could focus on the characters and write a new story about Max or the Wild Things. That would be interesting. But, we could even get more creative, and try writing about them in something other than a story or narrative format. For instance, we could write a poem about Max, or we could create a fictional television interview with him. We could write a missing-person report or do many other things. I want you to think about this story for awhile, in particular what was important for you, then take ideas from the original story and transform them into a new piece of writing. You have to be able to explain how your new piece and the original piece are connected, but you can be as creative as you like. What do you think?

Guided Practice: Multigenre writing projects are being used more frequently in secondary school literature and creative writing classes. These pieces of writing allow students to explore new genres as well as respond to an original story, play, or poem. In my writing workshops, I have had students take personal narratives that they have written and transpose them into poems, picture books, or news reports. These have been very successful writing experiences for my students, and have expanded their understandings of different genres.

Closing Comments: The real power of these lessons comes in the thinking required to take an original idea or theme and transpose it into a new genre. I strongly suggest to my students not to simply write a sequel, but rather to take a story or poem and transpose it into a new genre. Over the years, I have seen some truly unique responses to the original stories we have read and enjoyed. We are limited only by our imagination!

FIG. L7.3
Multigenre Possibilities

- ❖ eulogy for a character
- ❖ song
- ❖ poem
- ❖ greeting card
- ❖ résumé
- ❖ birth announcement for a character
- ❖ interview
- ❖ change setting
- ❖ advertisement
- ❖ change poem to story or story to poem

Books-to-Music Connections

The Challenge: Music plays a prominent role in the lives of many of our students. They have favorite musicians and, we hope, favorite authors as well. Listeners of popular music rarely investigate the meanings and lyrics of the songs they listen to. Many of the themes that are included in children's literature are also included in the songs they listen to. Understanding the connections between songs and stories helps readers develop more robust interpretations of both.

My Intentions: By having students make connections between the themes, ideas, and characters in songs and stories, I hope to help them attend to the important issues of their lives. All forms of art are open to interpretation—literature, painting, music, and theatre. I want readers to attend to the themes presented in various art forms and negotiate the meanings within our community of readers.

Lesson Overview: I will begin by demonstrating some connections between particular songs and some popular children's literature. I will discuss my connections and invite students to make some of their own.

How It Might Go: Good morning, Readers! I know that many of you spend a great deal of time listening to music. Do you ever listen to the lyrics and think about what the composer is trying to convey to you in your favorite songs? There are times when a particular song will remind me of a particular book. For example, when I first read *Pink and Say*, by Patricia Polacco (1994), I was reminded of an old song by the Band called *The Night They Drove Old Dixie Down*. You probably haven't heard of this band or this song because it's old, like me, but I typed up the words for you and have a recording of it. So, today after we read *Pink and Say*, we will listen to the song and see what connections arise.

Guided Practice: I invite students to include musical connections in their lit logs along with their literary and personal connections.

Closing Comments: Each day in my elementary classroom, we sing a song as I accompany my students on my guitar. Early in the year, I ask students to attend to the lyrics of each song, and we begin discussing what the lyrics of the song mean to us. For each song I choose, I try to present some context or explain some of the history of the song. I want students to discuss song lyrics in the same manner we discuss the books we read. Making connections to popular music provides another avenue to expand our responses and interpretations of literature.

Responding to Our Responses

The Challenge: When working with novice readers, we often focus on getting them to simply offer a response to what they are reading. We may use invested discussion strategies, like the ones described in this book, to help children respond to and interpret literature. What may go uninvestigated are the reasons for our particular responses. We need to ask ourselves and our students, "Why do we respond to texts the way we do?"

My Intentions: I want readers to begin to interrogate the ways they respond to texts and to analyze the patterns that arise in their literature response logs and literature study group discussions. In order to do so, we have to find ways to return to our initial responses and examine the ideas we had when we first encountered the text.

Lesson Overview: This series of lessons is designed to get readers to interrogate their responses to their reading and better understand themselves as readers. Using our literature response logs, any other written or artistic responses, and possibly some transcripts of literature study discussions, we will investigate how we respond to the different texts we read.

How It Might Go: Good morning, Readers! For quite some time now, we have been attempting to expand the way we respond to our reading. We have tried graffiti boards, artistic responses, discussion circles, and other invested discussion strategies. We have been writing impressions, connections, and wonderings in our literature response logs every night. Now, we are going to take a closer look at how we have been responding to our reading. What I want you to do is take out your literature response logs and closely examine some of the entries. Then, we are going to ask ourselves some questions I have developed. After we finish that investigation, we are going to listen to a literature study discussion that I recorded last week. I have typed up, or transcribed, some parts of that discussion, and we can take a look at that as well. We are trying to understand why we respond to literature the way that we do. Is it something about ourselves as readers that makes us respond a certain way, or is it the different experiences that we have had in our lives? Go get your lit logs and we will get started.

Guided Practice: I may share discussion transcripts with small groups of readers and ask them to analyze their discussions. Readers need a great deal of support in order to have this examination be successful. One way that has worked well for me has been to have students use Post-it notes to record ideas while they are reading a novel and then go back and analyze what they highlighted. They can write about what things they marked in the text and we can discuss what we are learning about ourselves as readers and how we respond to what we read.

Closing Comments: I would like to think that by doing these types of experiences, readers will begin to reflect more deeply about what they do when they are reading. This may not always be the case, but it is a worthy goal. There needs to be some lapse of time between the original responses and the reflection on these responses if readers are going to be able to step back and reflect on themselves as readers. Coming to understand how we respond to texts helps us make sense of what we are reading and also become aware of what kinds of readers we are.

FIG. L7.5
Analyzing Ourselves as Readers

After responding to a novel with Post-its, ask yourself:

❖ Did I pay attention to the character?

❖ Did I notice particular language?

❖ What did I mark the most? Funny events? Sayings?

❖ Did I mark things at the beginning, middle, or end the most?

❖ What things did I *not* mark at all?

❖ What patterns do I notice?

Evaluating Responses

The Challenge: Not all responses to literature are equally valid, are defendable, or lead to deeper or more sophisticated understandings. The problem we have is deciding what criteria we should apply to the types of responses we wish to evaluate. Too often, the criteria focus on literal recall and not on the qualities of more sophisticated responses, such as questions, connections, and inferences. I want readers to feel free to offer their ideas and feel comfortable sharing their thoughts with other readers. However, I also want readers to be able to defend their interpretations, provide sound reasoning for their thoughts, and negotiate meaning within our community of readers. This requires a certain amount of effort, to be accompanied with continued support for the readers in our community.

My Intentions: Using a framework I devised from a review of the literature on reader response theories and pedagogy, I will help readers evaluate the types of responses they construct with the literature they are reading.

Lesson Overview: Using our literature response logs, written responses to particular texts, or transcripts of literature discussions, we will analyze our responses based upon the criteria presented in Figure L7.6.

How It Might Go: Good morning, Readers! We have been reading and responding to different types of texts all year long. As we have been reading and discussing books, poems, plays, and song lyrics, I have tried to get you to think more deeply and critically about what you are reading. I think it is time that I share exactly what I expect of you as readers. Sophisticated readers do the following things. [Share criteria in Figure L7.6.] What I would like for us to do is use this list to try to expand the way we respond to what we are reading and see which ways are more difficult and which ones lead to better discussions and ideas. Some of the things on this list may sound quite familiar, like recalling ideas directly from the text. We do that all the time, don't we? However, some of the things on this list, for example, examining multiple perspectives with a text, may be quite new and challenging for us. I think that truly successful readers respond using a wide variety of perspectives and interpretive methods to understand what they are reading. Since our goal is to become better readers, and that means being better able to interpret and make sense of what we read, we will have to expand how we respond to what we are reading.

FIG. L7.6
Criteria for Evaluating Reader Responses

May be copied for classroom use.
© 2004 by Frank Serafini, from
Lessons in Comprehension.
Portsmouth, NH: Heinemann.

1. *Literal Recall*—Able to recall particular words or events from a story

2. *Aesthetic Engagement*—Able to relive characters' experiences, emotionally respond to a story, picture images in head, and follow along with a story, poem, or other text

3. *Intertextual Connections*—Able to make connections to other texts and experiences

4. *Multiple Perspectives*—Able to adopt other perspectives to a story, for example, examining the author's intentions, what the characters' motives might be, what our parents might think of a story, or whether girls and boys would respond differently to the story

5. *Analyze Response*—Able to reexamine one's own responses to a text

6. *Generate Interpretations*—Able to generalize meanings from texts to one's life experiences

7. *Evaluate Quality of the Piece of Literature*—Able to apply a set of literary criteria for analyzing the quality of a piece of literature

Guided Practice: Although I am not a proponent of using rubrics created outside the classroom, I am suggesting that the criteria I have proposed in Figure L7.6 may be used as a starting point for creating your own response evaluation rubric. This rubric should be used to expand responses, not to generate grades or demean readers.

Closing Comments: I will state firmly here, again, that this is *not* an assessment tool for determining levels of reader response, assigning grades for reading, or determining which book a particular reader should read. There are plenty of assessments that purport to do this already. What we need are assessment tools that go beyond simply leveling readers and readers' responses. My goal with this framework is to help readers expand their response repertoire, to help them adopt new ways to respond to a text. As readers expand the ways in which they are capable of responding to a text, they become more sophisticated readers and interpreters of literature. This is our goal as reading teachers.

Reader's Chair

The Challenge: Although we have come to include an Author's Chair as a way of responding to students' writing in our writing workshop, we rarely see examples of readers taking a Reader's Chair to discuss their interpretations of a text, the strategies they use when reading, the choices they make for reading, or the connections they construct during the reading workshop. What is often lost in comprehension instruction is an opportunity for readers to discuss how the lesson went or what strategies worked for them during the reading workshop. Reflection is a key ingredient in comprehension instruction—not just reflection on the teacher's part, but on the students', as well.

My Intentions: I want readers to be able to discuss the strategies they use and feel comfortable discussing their interpretations of particular pieces of literature. Each day, at the end of our reading workshop, I provide time for any reader to discuss how the lesson I provided helped or hindered his or her reading and understandings or discuss what was important for him or her.

Lesson Overview: I begin by demonstrating and discussing the concept of reader's chair. Each day after our reading workshop time, we gather around on the floor like we do after writing workshop, and students sign up to share their thoughts as readers.

How It Might Go: Good morning, Readers! What do we do at the end of every writing workshop? That's right, we have an Author's Chair. Well, I have been thinking that we should do the same when we finish our reading workshop. We should have a Reader's Chair. Each day, you can sign up and share some of your readings rather than your writings with the class. Let me sit in the Reader's Chair today and demonstrate what I mean.

I have been reading over all of the books by the author Colin Thompson. I think he is an excellent illustrator and author. I have noticed that he uses very detailed illustrations in his picture books. They almost look like the Where's Waldo? books because he hides things in the illustrations. He uses boys as the main characters all the time. There are some mysterious things going on in his books. This reminds me of Chris Van Allsburg's books. I think, if you like Van Allsburg, you would definitely like Colin Thompson.

So, how did that sound? Do you get the idea? You can share your ideas about books, authors, your reading strategies, today's lesson, anything you think is important about reading. There is a new sign-up sheet on the board and during reading workshop, if some great ideas come to you, just sign up. Okay?

Guided Practice: My hope is that we can use the Reader's Chair to help support readers in discussing books, authors, and their reading processes with each other. The language we use in Reader's Chair, and the demonstrations I provide, will help readers expand their understandings.

Closing Comments: The quality of readers' reflections and what gets shared during the Reader's Chair improves as the year progresses. In the beginning of the year, many readers simply share a favorite story or author or discuss a favorite part in a story. This is fine. As the year progresses, I demonstrate other things that can be shared in Reader's Chair and help students use this time to think and talk about themselves as readers. This is an important concept in developing a community of readers.

Reader Profile

The Challenge: In many elementary classes, the only person that evaluates students is the teacher. Student self-evaluation is seldom used. I think it is important for readers to think about themselves as readers, to examine the ways they respond to texts, and to interrogate these responses based on the criteria presented in Lesson 7.6. However, many novice readers have a difficult time reflecting on their own responses and reading processes.

My Intentions: In order to provide support for this type of analysis, or reflection, I have each reader interview and analyze another reader in our class. By examining how a different reader responds to texts and interprets books, readers may come to new understandings of themselves as readers.

Lesson Overview: I provide a series of questions and things to analyze for readers to develop a reader profile of another student in our class.

How It Might Go: Good morning, Readers! I have been asking you to think about yourselves as readers most of the year. We have looked at our literature response logs, analyzed our literature discussions, and shared our responses and comprehension strategies in the Reader's Chair. Well, I have another great idea. What if we tried to analyze another student in the class as a reader? What if I gave you a list of questions to ask someone and let you look at his or her literature response logs and asked you to develop what we are going to call a reader profile? A reader profile is a report on another person as a reader. When we are finished we will share our profile reports with the class. You will be introducing one of your friends as a reader. You can talk about what he or she likes, what he or she reads all the time, how he or she reads, where he or she reads, why he or she reads, and other important information. Sound interesting?

Guided Practice: Students will use the questionnaire provided (see Figure L7.8) and look at a reader's response log in order to complete the reader profile. I will work with individual students as they are gathering ideas and drawing conclusions.

FIG. L7.8
Reader Profile Questions

May be copied for classroom use.
© 2004 by Frank Serafini, from
Lessons in Comprehension.
Portsmouth, NH: Heinemann.

❖ What types of books does this person read the most?

❖ What types of books does this person not read very often?

❖ What does this person write about in his or her literature response log?

❖ What reading strategies does this person use?

❖ How many literature study groups has this person been in? Which books? What did he or she learn in the literature studies?

❖ Listen to the person read a picture book. What does he or she do while reading?

❖ Have the person do a think-aloud as he or she is reading a picture book. What does this person think about when he or she is reading?

❖ What things are hard for this reader?

❖ What things are easy for this reader?

❖ How can we help this student become a better reader?

Closing Comments: A great way to get this project going is to have another teacher or adult do a profile on you as a reader and present this to the class. We need to demonstrate what these profiles look like if they are going to be successful. I also allow time for the reader to add ideas about him- or herself during the profile report or presentation. The goal is to get readers to understand themselves as readers and to improve in any areas that need improvement.

Examining Critical Perspectives

For many reading theorists and educators, reading is no longer viewed as a solitary act involving innocent, naive readers and neutral, objective texts. For these theorists, texts are considered sociocultural artifacts, created by particular authors, with particular backgrounds, in particular times and contexts. Readers bring their histories and experiences to the reading of every text, in the same way writers bring their histories and experiences to the creation of texts. Critical perspectives focus on the political, social, cultural, and historical forces that affect readers as they construct meaning in transaction with texts. Helping readers interrogate these factors and the systems of power that influence the meanings we construct is the primary focus of this section.

Reading doesn't take place in a vacuum. The meanings that we construct as we read literature, expository texts, editorials, news reports, and presidential speeches are dependent on our understandings of the world and the culture and experiences we bring to the reading event. Because reading is no longer conceptualized as solely an individual act, we must begin to examine the forces and systems that affect the way we interpret texts, the meanings we construct, and how we negotiate those meanings in our community of readers. As readers learn *how* to read, they also come to define what reading *is*. This occurs in every classroom around the world. Our students come to understand what reading is by the expectations we set in our class and the experiences we provide for them with texts.

Critical literacy perspectives and activities encourage an awareness of how social practices affect the meanings we generate as readers. The lessons in this section enable readers to generate and analyze alternative interpretations of the texts we read and the meanings we take as normal or obvious. Instead of passively accepting the dominant interpretations or meanings, readers are taught to read against the grain, to disrupt their commonsense understandings and assume different perspectives when they are reading.

The comprehension lessons in this section include:

1. Uncovering Stereotypes
2. Understanding "Official" Meanings
3. Interrogating Advertisements
4. Asking New Questions
5. What We Used to Know
6. Analyzing the Classroom Library
7. Examining Magazines for Children
8. What Have They Done to This Story?

Uncovering Stereotypes

The Challenge: Novice readers need to understand that books are written from a particular perspective and that understanding this perspective is an important aspect of reading. Authors bring certain perspectives to their writing that may not align with the way readers see the world. Rather than having readers blindly accept the assumptions made by the author, we need to help readers read against the grain, that is, examine the perspectives that the author brings to the text and interrogate how these perspectives privilege or marginalize particular people. Uncovering stereotypes in literature helps develop critical readers and helps students understand that texts are social artifacts that have strong connections to the world in which we live.

My Intentions: This series of lessons is deigned to help students understand stereotypes in the literature they read and discuss how these affect us as readers. Using familiar characters, students will be able to discuss how gender is constructed in children's literature and how this may differ from our understandings of the real world.

Lesson Overview: I begin these lessons with students discussing the images and words that come to mind when they think of the character Cinderella. We make a list of Cinderella's character traits. Reading traditional versions of the Cinderella story, and then fractured and multicultural versions, we begin to uncover some of the stereotypes of women presented in many of the traditional versions.

How It Might Go: Good morning, Readers! How many of you know the story of Cinderella? [Many hands go up.] I thought so. I want you to think for a minute about what Cinderella was like in the traditional story. Let's make a chart of her traits (see Figure L8.1a). Okay, let's take a look at this chart. From what you said, it doesn't seem that Cinderella has very much control over her life. She is waiting for a prince and she gets pushed around a bit. Let me ask you one important question: Is this the way women act, or should act? Let's think about this as we read some Cinderella books from a different point of view (see Figure L8.1b).

Closing Comments: We use Cinderella to discuss the way in which gender is constructed in literature. We extend this discussion by cutting out images from magazines and newspapers of people we think are good-looking. This leads to interesting discussions about how we perceive men and women in our society. These lessons could also be done with books that contain familiar characters, for example, witches, wolves, or pigs. Using these familiar characters to begin with allows us an easy transition into interrogating stereotypes.

quiet

lonely

waiting for a prince

blonde with blue eyes

pretty, but hard to tell

helpful

kind to animals

does the cleaning

waits on her stepsisters

doesn't speak her mind

a pushover

treated poorly by her family

Cinder Edna, by Ellen Jackson

Cinder Elly, by Frances Minters

Dinorella, by Pamela Duncan Edwards

Yeh Shen, retold by Ai-Ling Louie

The Rough-Face Girl, by Rafe Martin

Prince Cinders, by Babette Cole

Cinderhazel, by Deborah Lattimore

Mufaro's Beautiful Daughters, by John Steptoe

The Paper Bag Princess, by Robert Munsch

Egyptian Cinderella, by Shirley Climo

The Turkey Girl, by Penny Pollock

Tattercoats, by Joseph Jacobs

Understanding "Official" Meanings

The Challenge: Whether we like it or not, most of our students will be required to take numerous standardized tests throughout their educational careers. Reader response theory may support instructional experiences and the way we respond to texts in the reading workshop, but a more objective, modernist theory of meaning is used to develop standardized reading tests. These tests require readers to find the main idea, identify predetermined meanings, and answer multiple-choice questions, primarily based on literal recall information. I want students to do well on these tests, of course, so I often discuss with students how to understand what the "official" meanings of a text may be. The challenge is to make sure we don't allow this form of reading to dominate reading experiences or allow all of our instructional experiences to simply prepare students to take tests. Reading to do well on standardized tests is simply *one* kind of reading, so we separate this approach to reading texts from others we use in the reading workshop.

My Intentions: This series of lessons is designed to help readers recognize what test makers look for and be able to summarize the major ideas of a text. I want readers to learn how to read to understand the official meanings of texts.

Lesson Overview: Using double-entry journals, I ask readers to record their impressions and connections on one side and what the test makers might ask about on the other side. We don't use these journals all year long; however, we use them in preparation for standardized tests.

How It Might Go: Good morning, Readers! In a few weeks, we will be taking standardized tests. Yes, I know you aren't looking forward to it. However, I have some ideas that we can use now that will help us prepare for them. I am going to ask you to take out your literature response logs (see Lesson 7.1), and we are going to use a different format for awhile. We are going to draw a line down the middle of a sheet of paper in the log. On one side of the paper we are going to put things we think the test makers may ask us about, and on the other we are going to put down things we care about, like impressions, connections, or wonderings. We are going to call the side of the paper with the test ideas Official Ideas. I want you to be able to recognize what the test makers might ask if the text you are reading was on a standardized test. We are going to talk about the kinds of things that test makers ask, but we are still going to talk about the things we care about and the connections we make to what we read. Unfortunately, test makers don't often ask readers to make connections or ask questions. This means that the way we read in reading workshop and the way we read for a standardized test are different. On the test, we are reading for one reason only: to answer the questions correctly. We are going to do this only for a few weeks before the test comes, but I think it will help us do better on the test. Are you ready to outsmart the test makers? Okay, let's get started.

Guided Practice: For a few weeks before the tests are given, the lit logs we use for homework change to the double-entry journals I have described. I want this part of test prep to be fun and not to diminish all the work we have done with understanding reading as a meaning-making process, where meanings are generated, shared, and negotiated in our community of readers. Students share their lit logs in the morning and discuss whether they were able to understand what the test makers might ask.

Closing Comments: These lessons are part of a unit of study on standardized tests as a genre. The passages on a standardized test are a particular genre that demand a different way of reading. I believe that attention to this way of reading for a short, intense period of time directly before the test will help our students do better. Teaching our readers how to understand the tricks and pitfalls of doing standardized tests, rather than explaining they just have to read better in general, does not change the way we read in the reading workshop or allow the tests to determine our reading curriculum.

Interrogating Advertisements

The Challenge: In our society, ignorance may be bliss, but it will cost you money in the long run. One place where this is especially apparent is in commercial advertising. Advertisers play on our innermost fears, suspicions, hopes, and dreams in order to sell us things. They also use stereotypes and cliché images to make us think that what they are presenting is the way things are. Although this is certainly difficult for young readers to understand, we need to begin to help them interrogate the images and ideas that are presented to us in advertisements and learn the ways advertisers are trying to persuade us to buy their products.

My Intentions: I want students to interrogate the way the world is presented in advertisements. Using commonly seen ads, we are going to deconstruct the images and slogans that appear in ads aimed at students to get them to buy certain back-to-school products. We will look at the way parents and children are portrayed and what we feel is important to buy for doing well in school.

Lesson Overview: Using newspaper advertisements for school supplies that regularly appear in August each year, these lessons are designed to help readers interrogate the images of children as students and adults as parents that appear in the ads. We will focus on school supplies; however, these lessons could be used with any advertisements, in any media.

How It Might Go: Good morning, Shoppers! That's right, shoppers. Today, we are going to look closely at some of those advertisements that come in the Sunday paper about what school supplies you should buy for going back to school. Let's look at this first ad about backpacks. Look at the kids in the picture. Do they look like you? What do you notice about them? Let's also look at what words are the biggest ones on the page. Why do you think the word *Sale* is so big? Let's take a look at the adults in the pictures. Do they look like your parents or adults you know? Let's discuss how they are similar and how they are different. Now, we can also look at what the particular products are in the ads and how they are trying to influence us.

Guided Practice: I give students various ads from the newspaper and ask them how the advertisers are trying to get their attention and what they are using to sell their products. I have them make lists of the words that are used and then we make a chart to see which words are used the most in these ads. These lessons may continue with television or radio ads. I often send students out to find ads about things they purchase regularly. I want them to understand how they may have been persuaded to buy these products. If possible, I may even find a marketing student or parent that works in advertising to come in and talk about how ads are created.

Closing Comments: My goal is not to undermine the work of advertisers. In some ways, they play an important role in our society, alerting people about what is being manufactured and sold. I just want students to learn how these ads work on us and whether we are being savvy shoppers when we purchase certain items. This is, of course, a very value-laden series of lessons. One person's trash is another one's treasure. However, if we learn how these advertisements work, and understand how they portray certain groups, we can make better decisions about the purchases we make.

Asking New Questions

The Challenge: Readers in school are socialized into particular ways of responding to texts, primarily because of the questions teachers and tests ask them and because of the expectations we have for readers and reading. Traditionally, teachers have used literal recall questions to determine whether a reader has comprehended a book that was read aloud or independently. These literal recall questions require readers to remember exact quotes or information from a text. This process may have more to do with memory than with understanding or comprehension. In order to support readers responding differently to texts, we may need to rethink the types of questions we ask them and the expectations we have for them as readers.

My Intentions: By demonstrating to readers a variety of questions that may be asked in conjunction with their reading and thinking and where the knowledge or information required to answer these various questions comes from, we may be able to change how readers approach a text, what they do to comprehend while they are reading, and the understandings they take away from the literary experiences we provide at school.

Lesson Overview: This series of lessons will show readers a variety of questions that can be posed before, during, and after reading. These questions will be organized into the following categories: text-based, author-based, reader-based, and context-based.

How It Might Go: Good morning, Readers! Have you ever noticed since you have been in school that when teachers finish reading a story to you, they usually ask you a lot of questions to see if you were paying attention or if you understood the story? [Discussion.] Usually, the kinds of questions the teacher asks are what we call literal recall questions. These kinds of questions focus on what is written exactly in the text. Instead of focusing on questions about the text itself, we could also ask questions about the author, what we think as readers, and how the text relates to what we know about the world. Let's make a chart with the words *Text, Author, Reader*, and *Context* on it, and I will show you what these different questions look like (see Figure L8.4).

Today, we are going to read the book *The Big Box*, by Toni and Slade Morrison (1999). When we are finished, we will ask some of each type of question and see how it changes what we think about and how we discuss the story.

FIG. L8.4
Categories of Questions

May be copied for classroom use.
© 2004 by Frank Serafini, from
Lessons in Comprehension.
Portsmouth, NH: Heinemann.

Text-Based

What is the main idea of the story?

What is the setting of the story?

Describe the main character.

Recall specific events of the story in sequence.

Author-Based

What is the author trying to tell you?

How did the author describe the character?

Reader-Based

What do you think this story is about?

How did you feel as you read the story?

What connections (personal or literary) did you make as you were reading?

Do the characters remind you of anyone?

How would you have acted if you were the main character?

How does the book relate to your life experiences?

Context-Based

Are any of the characters privileged or marginalized?

What attitudes or worldviews are endorsed or diminished?

What assumptions are taken for granted?

How are critical issues (race, gender, class, ethnicity) dealt with?

Is difference among people made visible?

Guided Practice: I might use these questions as prompts for class discussions or as literature response log categories.

Closing Comments: I want readers to learn to analyze literature from the four perspectives described in this section. I have been rethinking what I mean by *reading comprehension,* and one major component is certainly the ability to look at literature from a variety of perspectives. I will include a working definition of *reading comprehension* for you to think about: Reading comprehension is the ability or process of generating viable interpretations or meanings in transaction with text. This includes the ability to construct understandings from multiple perspectives, including author's intentions, textual references, personal experiences, and sociocultural influences.

What We Used to Know

The Challenge: There are many assumptions written about the world that often go unquestioned. Students read textbooks, Internet pages, and other resources and assume because it has been published, it must be true. Trying to get novice readers to not only comprehend what they are reading but question the assumptions made by the author is a challenge. When I grew up, we read history textbooks and simply memorized dates and names, assuming the information was factual. Now, we have begun to understand how every text, even nonfiction and history, has been written by someone who has a perspective and cultural, historical, and political agendas that affect what he or she writes.

My Intentions: Like all of the lessons in this section, the focus is on helping students learn to read against the grain, question sources and authors, and think about the relationship among what is being read, who wrote it, and what we know about the world.

Lesson Overview: By analyzing the information provided in older textbooks and comparing it with what we know now about specific topics, we can begin to discuss how perspective and context change what is written and what is understood. Taking the assumption "Columbus discovered America" as a starting point, we will look at a variety of sources and discuss whether this statement is "true."

How It Might Go: Good morning, Readers! Let's think back to what we talked about in our social studies lessons for a minute. I remember reading that Columbus discovered America, right? I would like to read a passage from an older history text that explains how Columbus discovered America. Then, we are going to read the book *Encounter*, by Jane Yolen (1992), and some of Columbus' journal entries. We will have to discuss how different versions of history support different ways of looking at the world. Let me ask you this question: Weren't people already living in the United States before Columbus discovered it? How can you discover some place where people already live? Next, we have to talk about who wrote the textbook and why they wanted to describe Columbus as the discoverer of America. Now, don't get me wrong, I'm not saying that Columbus wasn't a European who sailed across the Atlantic and landed near America. However, was he the first? Why did he get so much credit? We will have to read some different sources before we can address all of these questions.

Guided Practice: I usually have students go home and interview parents or neighbors about who they think discovered America. Ideas about the Vikings, Native Americans, Columbus, and others are usually uncovered. We discuss these various claims and use this questioning perspective to examine other historical "taken-for-granteds."

Closing Comments: The purpose of these lessons is to get students to realize that people with perspectives, biases, and different worldviews write textbooks and other texts. I want readers to begin to question what they read, not just learn to recall items from a text. The ability to question texts expands as readers learn more about the world, not just more about reading. I begin with the Columbus example because so much has been written about him from different perspectives. As we get going with this, I often bring in other examples from history texts about slavery, the Ku Klux Klan, and other controversial topics to present different perspectives for readers to examine. A democracy is built upon a questioning citizenry. Our reading programs should support this assumption.

Analyzing the Classroom Library

The Challenge: After teaching elementary school for many years and assembling a sizeable collection of children's literature and trade books, I began to notice that I tended to purchase books that had rebellious boys as the main characters. For those who know me, this may come as no surprise. I like adventure stories and gravitated to books with boys as protagonists. There were some books that included strong female characters, like Gilly Hopkins, Miss Rumphius, Brave Irene, and Salamanca Tree Hiddle. However, upon examination, it became apparent that I favored male characters.

Readers of all types should be able to see themselves in the books they read. How were some of my students going to be able to do this if my library didn't support the readers I had in my class? Since examining my library was a learning experience for myself, I felt that having students do the same thing might be helpful for them.

My Intentions: I want students to become aware of the types of books they select and what books are made available to them in classroom, school, and public libraries. By analyzing our classroom library, students will begin to recognize their reading preferences and any biases in the collections provided for them.

Lesson Overview: This series of lessons is designed to get students to recognize what characters, settings, and themes are in the books that were chosen for our classroom library. By counting the number of books with male and female characters, analyzing the numbers of books provided in each genre, and seeing if any groups of people or perspectives are left out, we can discuss who is missing and what books we may want to select for the library in the future.

How It Might Go: Good morning, Readers! The other day I was looking through the books on my shelves at my house and I realized that I liked certain kinds of books and didn't have certain other books. For example, I noticed that I didn't own many biographies, except those about musicians. I used to own a lot of horror books, but I don't buy many of them anymore. I like travel books and books about philosophy. I used to read Travis McGee mystery-adventure books but don't read any mysteries or thriller novels anymore. This made me wonder if the books I bought for our library were as one-sided as the books I bought at home. So, I took a look through and found a few things. I learned a lot by doing this and thought maybe we should take a look at our library, and maybe even the school library, to see what gets purchased and what doesn't. Let's start by looking at our list of genres that we have included in our library. Are there any important genres missing? I notice that we don't have many mysteries. Is this a problem? Do they publish fewer mysteries for children, or do I just not buy them because I don't read them at home? I think we need to take a look at what is in our library and make some suggestions about what we need to include that may be missing.

Guided Practice: One way to extend this lesson would be to take a look at the library orders for the past few years and see what kinds of books the school librarian usually orders. We could also have students go to bookstores or public libraries and analyze the best-seller lists or interview a librarian about what gets checked out the most. Circulation lists are easily made available and may add to our analysis.

Closing Comments: Since I did this examination of my library, I still like books with adventurous male characters, but I am cognizant of this preference and work hard to include both male and female characters in the novels I assign for literature studies in my college children's literature courses. I am not trying to change what readers read—we all have the right to choose books we like—but I want readers to understand what they may be missing.

Examining Magazines for Children

The Challenge: Although magazines make up a small percentage of classroom and school library collections, they are often the preferred reading materials for many novice readers, especially adolescents. With the extensive amount of advertising, self-help articles, and advice columns, these magazines often have an undue influence on readers' emerging identities and worldviews. Unfortunately, many agendas of the magazines' publishers and sponsors go unquestioned, possibly even unnoticed, by novice readers. Most readers view many of the ideas presented as natural or commonsensical. We need to help readers examine the way adolescents are portrayed, the way gender is constructed, and how commercial products are advertised if we want our children to become savvy consumers and responsible adults.

My Intentions: By examining one issue of a popular teen magazine, such as *Tiger Beat*, this series of lessons is designed to help demonstrate some reading strategies that readers can use to examine and question the material contained in magazines.

Lesson Overview: We will literally take apart a teen magazine and examine how it is structured, what sections it is composed of, how much advertising is included, what is being advertised and how, what topics are discussed, and how the authors and publishers of these magazines are persuading young readers to buy products and accept advice.

How It Might Go: Good morning, Readers! How many of you subscribe to a magazine at home or buy them at the bookstore? [Discussion.] Now, how many of you have ever analyzed what is in those magazines and what the advertisers and publishers do to get you to buy their magazines or their products? None of you? I thought so! Today, we are going to take apart an issue of *Tiger Beat* magazine and examine what is inside there. We are going to work in small groups to analyze particular sections of the magazine and then work as a whole group to look at the advertisements and layout of the magazine. We are not trying to make you stop buying these magazines, but we are trying to be better able to recognize how publishers and advertisers persuade you to buy things and the kinds of advice they offer teenagers. For example, we want to look at how the articles contained in the magazine represent young people. What do the kids in the ads and articles look like? How do they dress? What social classes and genders are represented? What messages are being conveyed to the readers? We need to look closely at these magazines to see how they may affect us as readers and as consumers. Let's take some of the analyzing strategies we have been working on and apply them to this magazine.

Guided Practice: I divide up the class into groups of two or three and give them a particular section of the magazine to read and analyze. We write down what we see and then ask some of the questions we have come up with as a class (see Figure L8.7). We use these small-group discussions to support our whole-group analysis of the magazines we read.

Closing Comments: Most classrooms do not focus on magazine reading. However, many adolescents and young adults read a variety of magazines as their primary reading material. Because of the commercial nature of magazine content, we need to help young readers analyze the intentions of the publishers and be able to critique what is included in the advertisements and advice columns.

FIG. L8.7
Questions for Examining Children's Magazines

May be copied for classroom use.
© 2004 by Frank Serafini, from
Lessons in Comprehension.
Portsmouth, NH: Heinemann.

1. What ages are the target audience for this magazine?
2. What are some messages aimed at boys in this magazine?
3. What are some messages aimed at girls?
4. What social classes, ethnicities, and races are represented in the illustrations?
5. What are the articles about?
6. What types of advice are offered readers?
7. What is being advertised? How?
8. How many pages of advertising versus reading material are there?
9. What images or stories can you relate to?
10. Which images or stories do you not relate to?
11. What do you think the publisher is saying about young people?
12. Would your parents agree with the publisher's ideas?

What Have They Done to This Story?

The Challenge: Whether we like it or not, commercial basal anthologies represent a large portion of the reading materials provided in elementary and middle school classrooms. Some researchers estimate that basals are in use in more than 90 percent of all American classrooms. What kinds of questions are asked in the teachers' manuals? What kinds of activities are included with each story? How are the stories abridged to fit into the anthology? Are illustrations or parts of the text left out?

Because basals are used in so many elementary classrooms, I believe they should be examined by both students and teachers for what is included and how reading lessons are created and structured. Teachers need to become decision makers, not merely program operators for implementing someone else's reading program.

The instructional plans and texts included in basal series may not be the same as the books we buy at the bookstore. We don't curl up by the fireplace, nor do we go on vacation, with a basal reader. We take authentic texts designed to tell stories or impart information to read when we sit on the beach or ride in a plane. There is a difference between trade books and commercial anthologies, in what is included and what is expected of readers. These differences need to be examined.

My Intentions: By examining what is included in a basal lesson, what a teachers' manual contains, and the way stories are abridged into anthologies, I want readers and teachers to understand the differences between these texts and the same stories included in trade books or authentic literature. The expectations that are created for readers when reading a story included in a basal are not the same as when a reader chooses a book from the library.

Lesson Overview: After I carefully choose several stories from the classroom basal anthology and the same stories published as trade books, we will examine what has been left out of the anthology and what activities and assessments have been included in the teachers' manual.

How It Might Go: Good morning, Readers! In some classrooms, teachers have a reading textbook, called a basal reader, to use to teach reading. Many of you have probably seen these in your student careers. These books are designed to help you become better readers, but the stories are sometimes shortened and some illustrations are left out. Today, we are going to look at one of our favorite stories, *Tacky the Penguin* (Lester 1990), and see how it looks in a basal reader compared with the actual book we have gotten used to reading. I borrowed a basal reader from another teacher so we could take a look at the story. Notice how some of the illustrations have been left out. There are a series of questions readers are supposed to answer when they are finished reading. Let's see if we can answer them.

Guided Practice: I gather up several basal readers from other classrooms, because I don't use one in my class, and allow students some time to look through and see what is in there. We make a chart listing the components of the basal we find, for example, discussion questions, extension activities, assessments, and reading guides. We discuss how these things may affect you as a reader and which ones may help you understand the story better. Students will surely encounter these texts somewhere in their school careers. It seems a worthwhile activity to explore how they expect readers to read.

Closing Comments: This lesson can be done with any story and any basal reader. Most basal series try to include the complete texts, but many are still abridged versions. I think it is important to examine what is included and see what is missing. The point of this lesson is not to bash the basal, but to make teachers and students aware of what is in their commercial textbooks.

FIG. L8.8
Questions to Ask About the Basal

May be copied for classroom use.
© 2004 by Frank Serafini, from
Lessons in Comprehension.
Portsmouth, NH: Heinemann.

❖ Have all of the illustrations been included?

❖ Has any of the text been changed?

❖ If any changes were made, why do you think they were made?

❖ What activities are included in the lessons?

❖ How do the activities relate to the story?

❖ What "official" meanings of the story are included in the teachers' manual?

❖ If your interpretations differ, why do they?

Epilogue

There is no single method of reading. T. S. Eliot once said that there was no method except to be very intelligent. I should prefer to say that, for most of us with middling gifts in the way of pure intelligence, serious attention to the craft of reading can take us quite far. Reading is the route to intelligence, not the goal of it. It is proper attention to the craft of reading that will make the reader crafty.

—ROBERT SCHOLES, *The Crafty Reader*

When I began teaching elementary school, I considered myself a whole language, progressive educator. After a few years, because of numerous misunderstandings concerning the basic tenets of whole language within the educational community and the general public, I would often describe myself as a balanced literacy teacher to avoid the negative connotations associated with the term *whole language*. It was just easier than explaining what I meant every time I said "whole language." Besides, it didn't send up as many red flares for people ignorant of whole language philosophy. It was politically less volatile to consider my reading program balanced, and it wasn't worth the trouble explaining what I meant by whole language. I even got to the point where I was reticent to tell people sitting next to me on long plane flights that I was a reading teacher. I didn't want to debate my way across the country.

In light of the political pressures and designs of the No Child Left Behind federal legislation, I have recently explained to audiences during workshops and conference presentations that I am an educator grounded in scientifically based reading research. Some groups have looked at me quite suspiciously for doing so, especially those educators who know my work, but I did it quite honestly. I have not been lying, nor have I been changing my beliefs to fit the newest political agenda. Although the labels I have used to describe my role in the classroom or my educational theories may have changed over the past few years, I haven't had to drastically change my teaching practices, nor my fundamental beliefs about literacy development, in order to align with these various labels. My teaching is, and has been, progressive, child-centered, balanced, and grounded in scientific research. I guess it just depends on whose version of scientific you are referring to.

When I began using a reading workshop approach, I taught comprehension strategies, invited readers to explore the structures and elements of literature, encouraged readers to make personal connections to the texts they read, and provided numerous opportunities for my students to discuss their responses to what they read. I also conducted comprehension lessons each day to help readers make sense of the texts they were reading. I did the same when I referred to myself as a whole language teacher, and as a balanced reading teacher, and I would do the same as a teacher grounded in scientifically based reading research.

The Road Ahead

It seems that everyone is concerned with the nature of the instructional reading experiences we offer our students, the scientific foundations upon which we base these experiences, how these instructional experiences will help readers develop their literate abilities, and how we plan to measure achievement and growth in reading proficiency. Given the pressures of adopting particular commercial reading programs by federal and state legislation, it has become apparent that we, as classroom teachers, need to be able to articulate the role direct or explicit comprehension instruction plays in our reading instruction framework. Does this mean that teachers have to follow the scope and sequence of a commercial reading program in order to ensure effective instruction? I don't believe so.

Although the search for the perfect reading program is fraught with pitfalls, it is important to analyze the criteria we use to distinguish exemplary reading instruction from poorly constructed reading instruction. Over the past three decades, there has been a shift back and forth from scripted, teacher-centered reading instruction lessons taken from commercial programs to student-centered comprehension lessons designed by classroom teachers and conducted within a reading workshop approach. Because of these shifts, the criteria used to evaluate what constitutes a quality lesson have had to change to align with new perspectives on reading instruction. The question remains, How do we know a quality comprehension lesson when we see one?

Reading instruction and literacy development aren't as neat and orderly as some commercial reading programs would like to portray. Effective classroom teachers know this. Parents of struggling readers know this. And, probably, struggling readers themselves know this. Ask any effective teacher if teaching readers to make sense of what they are reading is as easy as following a set of scripted lessons and you will hear a resounding "No!" Teachers who teach reading know that effective comprehension instruction is a complicated process that involves a vast array of instructional components, procedures, and considerations.

Throughout this text, I have started each lesson with the comment "Good morning, Readers!" I have done so deliberately and with strong convictions. Like Robert Scholes said in this section's epigraph, it is attention to the craft of reading that will make the reader crafty, not some innate, cognitive endowment. This statement gives hope to teachers of reading. Young people become better readers by reading. No matter what cognitive capacities they bring to the reading event, practicing reading makes them better readers. I believe that students rise to our expectations. If we see them as readers and treat them as readers, they will come to see themselves as readers, and from then on there is no stopping them.

In a society that desires fast food over quality nutrition, it should come as no surprise that we skim along the top of the reading curriculum. District, state, and federal curriculum guidelines mandate additional requirements to an already overburdened reading curriculum. As teachers, we are told we need to teach faster and harder every day if we expect to see results. How unfortunate—and absurd. The expansion of the reading curriculum forces teachers to sacrifice depth of understanding for coverage of specific topics. Our reading curricula have become a trivial pursuit for trivial knowledge.

It may seem counterintuitive for me to be calling for teachers to slow down and revisit books again and again throughout the year. Several of the comprehension lessons included in this text require teachers to return to favorite and familiar titles to allow students to develop new interpretations, new comprehension practices, and deeper understandings. I hope teachers see the value in this proposal. If we keep forcing readers to read only books they haven't seen before, instead of allowing them to revisit favorites from time to time, we are denying them access to the multiple layers of meaning that can be generated during additional transactions with quality literature.

Novice readers come to understand what reading *is* as they come to understand *how* to read. Reading is a lifelong process of making sense of the world and our place in it. It is not a rush to finish books, nor to accumulate reading trophies by answering five questions on some computer quiz. Our teaching must convey this message as much as it helps readers learn to read. If we don't help readers understand *why* they should read, they won't care about learning *how* to do it.

Professional References

Allington, Richard L., and Sean A. Walmsley, eds. 1995. *No Quick Fix: Rethinking Literacy Programs in America's Elementary Schools*. New York: Teachers College Press.

Bomer, Randy. 1998. "Transactional Heat and Light: More Explicit Literacy Learning." *Language Arts* 76 (1): 11–18.

Cambourne, Brian. 1988. *The Whole Story: Natural Learning and the Acquisition of Literacy in the Classroom*. Auckland, NZ: Ashton Scholastic.

———. 1999. "Explicit and Systematic Teaching of Reading: A New Slogan?": *The Reading Teacher* 53 (2): 126–27.

Durkin, Dolores. 1979. "What Classroom Observations Reveal About Reading Comprehension Instruction." *Reading Research Quarterly* 14: 481–533.

Freire, Paulo, and Donaldo Macedo. 1987. *Literacy: Reading the Word and the World*. South Hadley, MA: Bergin and Harvey.

Hoyt, Linda, Margaret Mooney, and Brenda Parkes. 2003. *Exploring Informational Texts: From Theory to Practice*. Portsmouth, NH: Heinemann.

Keene, Ellen O., and Susan Zimmermann. 1997. *Mosaic of Thought: Teaching Comprehension in a Reader's Workshop*. Portsmouth, NH: Heinemann.

Langer, Ellen. 1997. *The Power of Mindful Learning*. Reading, MA: Addison-Wesley.

Moss, Barbara. 2003. *Exploring the Literature of Fact: Children's Nonfiction Trade Books in the Elementary Classroom*. New York: Guilford.

Pearson, P. David, and M. C. Gallagher. 1983. "The Instruction of Reading Comprehension." *Contemporary Educational Psychology* 8: 317–44.

Pennac, Daniel. 1999. *Better Than Life*. Markham, Ontario: Pembroke.

Peterson, Ralph. 1992. *Life in a Crowded Place: Making a Learning Community*. Portsmouth, NH: Heinemann.

Pressley, Michael, and Cathy Collins Block. 2001. *Comprehension Instruction: Research-Based Best Practices*. New York: Guilford.

Pressley, Michael, Cathy Collins Block, and Linda Gambrell. 2002. *Improving Comprehension Instruction: Rethinking Research, Theory, and Classroom Practice*. Indianapolis: Jossey-Bass.

Price, Deborah P. 1998. "Explicit Instruction at the Point of Use." *Language Arts* 76: 19–26.

Scholes, Robert. 2001. *The Crafty Reader*. New Haven, CT: Yale University Press.

Serafini, Frank. 2001. *The Reading Workshop: Creating Space for Readers*. Portsmouth, NH: Heinemann.

Snow, Catherine, and Anne Sweet. 2003. *Rethinking Reading Comprehension*. New York: Guilford.

Wood, Diane, Jerome Bruner, and G. Ross. 1976. "The Role of Tutoring in Problem Solving." *Journal of Child Psychology and Psychiatry* 17: 89–100.

Children's Literature References

Ahlberg, Allan, and Janet Ahlberg. 1986. *The Jolly Postman, or, Other People's Letters*. New York: Little, Brown.

Anno, Mitsumasa. 1978. *Anno's Journey*. New York: Putnam.

Babbitt, Natalie. 1994. *Bub, or, the Very Best Thing*. New York: HarperCollins.

Banyai, Istvan. 1995. *Zoom*. New York: Viking.

Base, Graeme. 1989. *The Eleventh Hour*. New York: Abrams.

———. 1996. *The Discovery of Dragons*. New York: Abrams.

Bloom, Becky. 1999. *Wolf*. New York: Orchard.

Briggs, Raymond. 1999. *The Snowman*. New York: Random House.

Browne, Anthony. 1990. *Changes*. London: Julia MacRae.

———. 1991. *Willy's Pictures*. Cambridge, MA: Candlewick.

———. 1992. *Zoo*. New York: Knopf.

———. 1998. *Voices in the Park*. New York: DK.

Bunting, Eve. 1999. *Night of the Gargoyles*. New York: Clarion.

Burningham, John. 1999. *John Patrick Norman McHennessy: The Boy Who Was Always Late*. Wethersfield, CT: Dragonfly.

Clement, Rod. 1995. *Just Another Ordinary Day*. New York: Scholastic.

———. 1998. *Grandpa's Teeth*. New York: HarperCollins.

Climo, Shirley. 1989. *Egyptian Cinderella*. New York: Crowell.

Cole, Babette. 1988. *Prince Cinders*. New York: Putnam.

Coleman, Evelyn. 1999. *White Socks Only*. Morton Grove, IL: Whitman.

Crew, Gary. 1999. *The Watertower*. Northampton, MA: Interlink.

Cronin, Doreen. 2000. *Click, Clack, Moo: Cows That Type*. New York: Simon and Schuster.

dePaola, Tomie. 1978. *Pancakes for Breakfast*. Orlando: Harcourt.

Dr. Seuss. 1960. *Green Eggs and Ham*. New York: Random House.

Eastman, P. D. 1960. *Are You My Mother?* New York: Random House.

Edwards, P. D. 1999. *Dinorella*. New York: Hyperion.

Egan, Tim. 1999. *Metropolitan Cow*. New York: Houghton Mifflin.

Everitt, Betsy. 1992. *Mean Soup*. Orlando: Harcourt.

Fox, Mem. 1994. *Koala Lou*. New York: HarperCollins.

———. 1997. *The Straight Line Wonder*. New York: Mondo.

———. 2002. *Feathers and Fools*. New York: HarperCollins.

Freeman, Mae. 1971. *You Will Go to the Moon*. New York: Random House.

Gibbons, Gail. 1997. *The Moon Book*. New York: Holiday House.

Goss, Linda. 1996. *The Frog Who Wanted to Be a Singer*. New York: Orchard.

Guarino, Deborah. 1997. *Is Your Mama a Llama?* New York: Scholastic.

Henkes, Kevin. 1996. *Lily's Purple Plastic Purse*. New York: Greenwillow.

Howe, James. 1999. *Horace and Morris, but Mostly Dolores*. Orange, CA: Atheneum.

Jackson, Ellen. 1994. *Cinder Edna*. New York: Lothrop Lee and Shepard.

Jacobs, Joseph. 1989. *Tattercoats*. New York: Putnam.

Joyce, William. 1995. *Dinosaur Bob and His Adventures with the Family Lazardo*. New York: HarperCollins.

———. 2001. *Santa Calls*. New York: HarperCollins.

Lattimore, Deborah Nourse. 1997. *Cinderhazel: The Cinderella of Halloween*. New York: Scholastic.

Legge, David. 1995. *Bamboozled*. New York: Scholastic.

Lester, Helen. 1990. *Tacky the Penguin*. New York: Houghton Mifflin.

Lichtenheld, Tom. 2003. *What Are You So Grumpy About?* New York: Little, Brown.

Lorbiecki, Mary Beth. 2000. *Sister Anne's Hands*. New York: Puffin.

Louie, Ai-Ling. 1982. *Yeh Shen: A Cinderella Story from China*. New York: Putnam.

Macauley, David. 1987. *Why the Chicken Crossed the Road*. Boston: Houghton Mifflin.

———. 1990. *Black and White*. Boston: Houghton Mifflin.

———. 1995. *Shortcut*. Boston: Houghton Mifflin.

———. 1997. *Rome Antics*. Boston: Houghton Mifflin.

MacQuilty, Miranda. 1994. *Desert*. New York: Knopf.

Marsden, John. 2001. *The Rabbits*. Melbourne: Lothian.

Martin, Jacqueline Briggs. 1998. *Snowflake Bentley*. New York: Houghton Mifflin.

Martin, Rafe. 1992. *The Rough-Face Girl*. New York: Philomel.

Mayer, Mercer. 1968. *There's a Nightmare in My Closet*. New York: Dial.

McDermott, Gerald. 1974. *Arrow to the Sun: A Pueblo Indian Tale*. New York: Viking.

McKee, David. 1989. *Elmer*. New York: HarperCollins.

McPhail, David. 1997. *Edward and the Pirates*. New York: Little, Brown.

Miller, William. 1998. *The Bus Ride*. New York: Lee and Low.

Minters, Frances. 1994. *Cinder Elly*. New York: Viking.

Morrison, Toni, and Slade Morrison. 1999. *The Big Box*. New York: Jump Sun.

Munsch, Robert. 1980. *The Paper Bag Princess*. Toronto: Annick.

O'Neill, Alexis. 2002. *The Recess Queen*. New York: Scholastic.

O'Neill, Mary. 1989. *Hailstones and Halibut Bones*. New York: Doubleday.

Paulsen, Gary. 1993. *Nightjohn*. New York: Delacourt.

Pinkwater, Daniel. 1993. *The Big Orange Splot*. New York: Scholastic.

Polacco, Patricia. 1994. *Pink and Say*. New York: Philomel.

Pollock, Penny. 1995. *The Turkey Girl: A Zuni Cinderella Story*. New York: Little, Brown.

Raschka, Chris. 1993. *Yo! Yes?* New York: Orchard.

———. 2001. *Table Manners*. Boston: Candlewick.

Rathmann, Peggy. 1995. *Officer Buckle and Gloria*. New York: Putnam.

Rosen, Michael. 1998. *This Is Our House*. Boston: Candlewick.

Say, Allen. 1993. *Grandfather's Journey*. New York: Houghton Mifflin.

———. 1995. *Stranger in the Mirror*. New York: Houghton Mifflin.

———. 2002. *Home of the Brave*. New York: Houghton Mifflin.

Scieszka, Jon. 1993. *The Stinky Cheese Man and Other Fairly Stupid Tales*. New York: Viking.

———. 1996. *The True Story of the Three Little Pigs*. New York: Puffin.

Sendak, Maurice. 1963. *Where the Wild Things Are*. New York: HarperCollins.

———. 1993. *We Are All in the Dumps with Jack and Guy*. New York: HarperCollins.

Shannon, David. 1999. *David Goes to School*. New York: Blue Sky.

Sharmat, Marjorie Weinman. 1980. *Gila Monsters Meet You at the Airport*. New York: Simon and Schuster.

Sis, Peter. 1996. *Starry Messenger*. New York: Farrar, Straus and Giroux.

———. 1998. *Tibet: Through the Red Box*. New York: Farrar, Straus and Giroux.

Slobodkina, Esphyr. 1985. *Caps for Sale*. New York: HarperCollins.

Smith, Lane. 1988. *Flying Jake*. Orange, CA: Atheneum.

———. 1995. *Glasses: Who Needs 'Em?* New York: Puffin.

Snow, Alan. 1995. *How Dogs Really Work*. New York: Little, Brown.

Steig, William. 1972. *Dominic*. New York: Farrar, Straus and Giroux.

———. 1976. *Abel's Island*. New York: Farrar, Straus and Giroux.

———. 1982. *Doctor DeSoto*. New York: Farrar, Straus and Giroux.

———. 1984. *Yellow and Pink*. New York: Farrar, Straus and Giroux.

———. 1985. *Solomon the Rusty Nail*. New York: Farrar, Straus and Giroux.

———. 1986. *Brave Irene*. New York: Farrar, Straus and Giroux.

———. 1988. *Sylvester and the Magic Pebble*. New York: Simon and Schuster.

Steptoe, John. 1997. *Mufaro's Beautiful Daughters*. New York: Lothrop, Lee and Shepard.

Stevens, Janet. 1995. *Tops and Bottoms*. Orlando: Harcourt.

St. George, Judith. 2000. *So You Want to Be President?* New York: Philomel.

Thompson, Colin. 1993. *Looking for Atlantis*. New York: Knopf.

Trivizas, Eugene. 1997. *Three Little Wolves and the Big Bad Pig*. New York: Aladdin.

Turner, Ann. 1995. *Nettie's Trip South*. New York: Aladdin.

Van Allsburg, Chris. 1979. *The Garden of Abdul Gasazi*. Boston: Houghton Mifflin.

————. 1981. *Jumanji*. Boston: Houghton Mifflin.

————. 1986. *The Stranger*. Boston: Houghton Mifflin.

————. 1995. *Bad Day at Riverbend*. Boston: Houghton Mifflin.

————. 2002. *Zathura*. Boston: Houghton Mifflin.

Whitcomb, Mary E. 1998. *Odd Velvet*. San Francisco: Chronicle.

Wiesner, David. 1991. *Tuesday*. New York: Clarion.

————. 1992. *June 29, 1999*. New York: Clarion.

————. 1999. *Sector 7*. New York: Clarion.

————. 2001. *The Three Pigs*. New York: Clarion.

Willard, Nancy. 1991. *Pish, Posh, Said Hieronymus Bosch*. San Diego: Harcourt.

Wisniewski, David. 1998. *The Secret Knowledge of Grown-Ups*. New York: Lothrop, Lee and Shepard.

Wood, Audrey. 1990. *I'm as Quick as a Cricket*. Wiltshire, UK: Child's Play.

————. 1992. *Silly Sally*. Orlando: Harcourt.

————. 1996. *Bright and Early Thursday Evening*. Orlando: Harcourt.

Yolen, Jane. 1987a. *Owl Moon*. New York: Philomel.

————. 1987b. *Piggins*. Orlando: Harcourt.

————. 1988. *Picnic with Piggins*. Orlando: Harcourt.

————. 1992. *Encounter*. Orlando: Harcourt.

Young, Ed. 1992. *Seven Blind Mice*. New York: Philomel.